A GUIDE TO THE INDUSTRIAL
BY MALCOL

E

125: Lamb's brick works, South Godstone

Photo: Chris Shepheard

INTRODUCTION

Readers in Tandridge District may be forgiven for being surprised that their district has an industrial history at all. The essential charm of the district, and the reason many settle there, is that it is a rural area which was seemingly bypassed by the industrial revolution. Thoughts of the district are likely to turn to hills, woods, meadows, streams and delightful old cottages and manor houses. The very thought of equating these gentle rustic delights with the harshness of industry is disturbing.

But the sand pits and the fuller's earth pits south of the North Downs, now mostly land-fill sites, tell a different story. So do the railways and the roads and the array of aerials at the crest of the North Downs. The arrival of the railways produced new and large centres of population at Oxted, Caterham and Whyteleafe and created smaller villages at South Godstone and South Nutfield. Industries, light and heavy, came into being. These include coal yards, brickworks, limeworks and chemical works.

Long before the arrival of the railways and good roads, various pits and ponds recall the Wealden iron industry, the fuller's earth industry and the gunpowder industry at Godstone. Numerous windmills and water mills recall the basic industry of corn grinding.

This book is a work of history based on industrial archaeology. That is to say, it is history based on industrial features of the landscape which can be seen or (with the proviso that most are on private property and may require permission) visited.

In the 1960s industrial archaeology began to develop as a subject separate from main-stream archaeology and over the years has assimilated a great many disparate topics ranging from nuclear power stations to ornamental wrought iron work. Many people, including this author, argue that industrial archaeology cannot be precisely defined and therefore in choosing topics for this book the criterion has been, that the topics have been talked about by some industrial archaeologists at some time. This includes 19th and 20th century military structures. Since the time of the American Civil War a nation's ability to devise, manufacture and deliver weapons and defensive systems in large quantities has been a more significant factor in winning a war than purely military considerations.

It is regretted that the subject matter of this book is incomplete. For various reasons a study of the numerous small businesses, such as light engineering firms, many of which are virtually hidden away in villages, await a later publication. Included with this are developments at such places as Hurst Green and Redhill aerodrome and more recently little computer firms and offices which are being set up in old farm houses.

In conclusion Tandridge District can take pride in, at times, playing a leading role in the nation's scientific and technical achievements. The first Astronomer Royal was Rector of Burstow; important technical innovations were effected by Fuller's Earth Union; pioneering work in the field of telecommunications occurred at Tatsfield; the construction of the Caterham bypass was an important occasion in the history of road building; the first concrete house may have been built at Caterham on the Hill; and without Kenley Aerodrome the Battle of Britain in 1940 may not have been won.

THE TOPOGRAPHY OF TANDRIDGE

The geology of the district has caused a wide variation in the landscape throughout a small area. For example there is little resemblance between the dry plateau land at Tatsfield, the heath land at Limpsfield Chart and the 'East Anglian' scenery in the Eden Valley.

In turn the industrial and residential development has been influenced by the landscape and geological factors.

To the north there is the dip slope of the North Downs which slopes gently towards the population centre of Croydon and it constitutes a plateau land intersected with dry valleys. The plateau consists of chalk largely capped with clay-with-flints.

The scarp face of the North Downs presents a wall between the Vale of Holmesdale and the plateau land which leads to London. The only significant road across it is the A22 at Godstone. All other roads are steep and sunken between high banks. The scarp face has been exploited for chalk, and the Upper Greensand strata at its base for firestone and hearthstone.

The underlying very sticky Gault Clay, followed by the Folkestone beds of the Lower Greensand constitutes the Vale of Holmesdale which has been raped by the M25. The Folkestone beds have been exploited for sand and water. The Lower Greensand rises up to form the ridge on the south side of the Vale of Holmesdale. It is an important ridge since it forms a dry east-west causeway between the clays north and south of it. Therefore we find the main road and Nutfield, Bletchingley, Godstone, Oxted and Limpsfield along its length. It has been exploited for fuller's earth in the Sandgate Beds and, on the south face, for stone in the Hythe Beds. Particularly between Redhill and Godstone it forms a barrier between London and the Weald and is crossed by narrow sunken lanes. The M23 is a brutal insertion.

To the south of the Greensand ridge and its underlying Atherfield Clay lies the flat area of the Wealden clay which is interrupted by small ridges of sandstone, particularly at Outwood, but which stretches to Felbridge where it meets the sands of the High Weald and to Smallfield where it meets river gravels. Most of it is drained by the river Eden to the east but some to the west by the river Mole.

2

36: Oxted railway viaduct   *Photo: Chris Shepheard*

II: Wapses Lodge roundabout, Caterham bypass   *Photo: Chris Shepheard*

M23 AND M25

TQ 304 537 to TQ 309 427 and TQ 306 533 to TQ 429 546

The most important of the roads passing through Tandridge District are the M23 and the M25 motorways which were constructed in the early 1970s. The purpose of the M25 was to form a ring road around London but in recent times has been found inadequate and in 1993 there were proposals to widen it and incorporate extra traffic lanes.

The original purpose of the M23 is more obscure. As originally conceived it was to connect with motorways in London but when built was simply terminated, at its northern end, on the London to Brighton road at Hooley. It failed as a London to Brighton road by being terminated at Pease Pottage at its southern end. In 1993 a massive engineering project upgrading the A23 from Pease Pottage to Brighton to motorway standards in effect completed a motorway from Hooley to Brighton and connected Brighton to the nationwide motorway network by means of the M25.

The M23 was successful from its outset at incorporating Gatwick Airport in the motorway network. Both the motorways caused immense environmental damage to Tandridge District and destroyed archaeological sites during construction. Included in this was damage to very precious ancient underground stone quarries (**site 106**, TQ 307 537) near the intersection of the motorways.

There are impressive civil engineering features associated with the motorways.

1 INTERSECTION OF M23 AND M25 WARWICK WOLD

TQ 307 533   ✱

Built in the early 1970s, the opening of this construction was delayed owing to the abandonment of work on the M25 for a short period when the contractors, French, went out of business.

2 A25 BRIDGE OVER THE M23 BETWEEN NUTFIELD AND BLETCHINGLEY

TQ 315 508   ✱

This very elegant concrete and steel bridge carries the A25 over possibly the deepest

motorway cutting in the country. A deposit of fuller's earth was uncovered while it was being dug.

3-6 THE A22

TQ 337 590 to TQ 373 396   ✱

Before the motorways the most important roadway through Tandridge District was that through the gap in the North Downs north of Godstone which has evolved to the present A22.

It was turnpiked in 1718 and by the early 19th century it had become the first recognised **3** London to Brighton road. Coaches used it during the 19th century but a motor bus service connecting Brixton to Whyteleafe (Sundays only) was established in 1912. Buses reached Godstone (Stockwell to Godstone - Sundays only) in 1913. Godstone bus station (**site 4**, TQ 350 522) was built in 1925 but it was the property of East Surrey Traction Company which had started services from Reigate to Godstone in 1914.

A Green Line service (East Grinstead, Godstone and Oxford Circus) was established in 1930 but at the time it was in competition with another company, Blue Belle, which established a similar service in the same year.

Changing fashions in operating bus services were demonstrated by the demolition of Godstone bus station during February-March 1993 after a period of disuse. Chelsham bus station (**site 5**, TQ 365 583) was demolished a year or two previously.

A toll house on the west side of Wapses Lodge roundabout (**site 6**, TQ 346 572) recalls the coaching days.

7 LIMPSFIELD TO CROYDON via TITSEY ROAD

TQ 408 527 to TQ 349 596 ✳

An alternative route across the North Downs was the Limpsfield to Titsey road which, although it acquired sufficient status to be turnpiked in 1813, was too steep to evolve to importance in modern times. It is near the line of the second Roman road (London to Lewes), which passes through the district. Part of the route of the Roman road has been incorporated into Clarks Lane and Rectory Lane. Excavations for the Clacket Lane service station on the M25, 1992-1993, uncovered a section.

A toll house survives–Paygate Cottage on Botley Hill, (**site 8**, TQ 394 557).

9 ROMAN ROAD, GODSTONE GAP

TQ 351 541 ✳

The original London to Portslade Roman road passed through the Godstone gap in the North Downs but at some time during the 19th century the road, as we know it today (A22), acquired a line a short distance to the west, through the area then being worked for chalk and firestone. The original Roman road still exists as a sunken track.

An act of 1585 indicates that the road was carrying iron and charcoal from the Weald and that the carriers had to cart loads of stone to repair the road they were using and damaging.

As it proceeded northwards the Roman road passed over Riddlesdown which is on the east side of the Caterham valley. The decline in the use of this section of the road began in about 1790 when a new road was built from Purley to the *Rose and Crown* in Kenley.

10-11 CATERHAM BYPASS AND WAPSES LODGE ROUNDABOUT

TQ 347 546 to 346 572 ✳

These were constructed in 1939. *The Daily Telegraph* of 10 March 1939 recorded that the roundabout (**site 11**, TQ 346 572) was the first of its kind to be constructed in this country. Its interesting features are the pedestrian subways which pass under the six converging roads into the open submerged centre of the roundabout.

The *Croydon Advertiser* intimated on 14 April 1939 that the bypass was first used on 7 April 1939. There was no ceremonial opening.

During WWII, because the roundabout was white and therefore visible from the air, it was camouflaged with netting and tree branches mounted on scaffold poles and also by planting fir trees. The bypass itself was tarred and patterned with two different coloured grits. Unfortunately this could not have been altogether successful because allied airmen used the roundabout as a navigational aid. A route from the Straits of Dover, was to follow the railway through Ashford and along the Tonbridge line to Godstone station. To reach Kenley they turned right at Godstone station and left at the roundabout.

The pedestrian subways at the roundabout were used as air-raid shelters.

It was not until 1967 that the road from Wapses Lodge roundabout to Whyteleafe South station was made into a dual carriage way. In about 1970 the A22 south of the Caterham bypass was made into a dual carriageway almost to Godstone.

12-13 GODSTONE BYPASS

TQ 352 527 to TQ 363 503 ✳

In 1972-3 the Godstone bypass was constructed to divert the A22 to the east side of the village. This afforded the opportunity to establish that the Roman Road was intersected by the northern end of the bypass near where the A22 now enters the roundabout, (**site 13**, TQ 351 529).

14 SALT ROUTE

The house known as the 'Salt Box' (**TQ 421 518** ■) which stands on the Kent Hatch Road

(B269) a short distance west of the **Carpenter's Arms** was rebuilt in the nineteenth century.

There is another 'Salt Box' at Biggin Hill. This allied to the fact that they are both not too far from the course of the Roman Road, which runs from quite near Saltdean on the Sussex Coast, has led to the belief that a 'salt road' is indicated. If this is true the salt would have been obtained by the evaporation of sea water.

A further claim is that the narrow Greensand ridge on which the Salt Box stands would have been a conveniently dry spot for the former salt storehouse.

2   RAILWAYS

Tandridge District has three railway lines; the Tonbridge line, the Caterham Line and the Oxted line. No main line railways have been closed but there were once tiny light railways connected with chalk pits, clay pits and stone quarries. These no longer exist.

15 THE TONBRIDGE LINE
TQ 290 494 to 383 481   ■

The line from Redhill to Tonbridge, the first main line to Dover, was one of the first railways to be built and when extended to Folkestone eventually afforded a means for the wealthy to travel to the continent and in particular Paris. But this had to await the development of Folkestone Harbour and of railways in northern France both backed by the South-Eastern Railway Company

The line from Redhill to Tonbridge, which was constructed starting at Tonbridge, was opened 26 May 1842 and officially opened to Folkestone 24 June 1843. (Opened to public on 28 June). Dover was reached in February 1844.

The extension to Reading (1849) was to prove useful after the War Office instigated the building of army camps near Aldershot (1854). From then on soldiers could be carried to the channel ports quickly.

Also the line was able to carry holiday makers from the Midlands to the resorts of Kent without crossing London.

In 1898 the company, the South Eastern Railway, formed a working union with the London Chatham and Dover Railway and the line then became under the control of the South Eastern and Chatham railway.

Sir Edward Watkin the rude and aggressive 'Railway King' with grandiose ideas became chairman of the SER Board in 1866 and retired in 1894 to the relief of the shareholders and the Stock Exchange. One of his dreams was to connect Manchester to the northern shores of France by a Channel Tunnel. The SER started the tunnel in 1882 by sinking a shaft at Shakespeare Cliff but for reasons of national security the government stopped the project.

By 1993, the Channel Tunnel had been completed and preparations were in an advanced stage for the electrification and upgrading of the Tonbridge line. When complete Channel Tunnel trains will pass through Tandridge district several times each hour 24 hours a day. Noise barriers will be erected at places such as South Nutfield.

The Tonbridge line through Tandridge District is notable for being very straight. It is claimed the engineer for the line, Sir William Cubitt, took his sighting from what is now the view-point on Redhill Common. Nevertheless a tunnel had to be constructed in the southern part of Bletchingley Parish. The Blechingley Tunnel. (Bletchingley is now spelled with a 'T' but was not at the time the tunnel was built.)

16 BLETCHINGLEY TUNNEL
TQ 332 488 to 344 486   ■

This tunnel is 1,200m long, is brick-lined and was built by Frederick Walter Simms who had to contend with the considerable problems of waterlogged and faulted Weald Clay which also contained a mass of detached sandstone rock.

It was built using twelve shafts and was opened to the public on 26 May 1842.

Unusually, for a tunnel, Simms published a **5**

16: Bletchingley tunnel   *Photo: Chris Shepheard*

book, *Practical Tunnelling*, 1844, (2nd edition 1860) describing the construction of the tunnel in detail. This went into a total of four editions during the century, and was for much of that time the standard work on tunnelling.

17 NAVVY CAMP
TQ 327 487   ■

The canteen for the railway navvies was attached to the house opposite Kennels Farm in Outwood Lane. Although work on the tunnel resulted in the assembly of the largest body of men working on railways in the south east of England in 1840-1842 it is believed that they were largely locally recruited. The 1841 census reveals that Irish navvies would have been in the minority.

18 SOUTH NUTFIELD VILLAGE AND STATION
TQ 305 491   ✳

The financial collapse of the bank Overend Gurney in 1866 caused its principal shareholder H E Gurney to have to sell his property to the south of Nutfield village. At least some of this was purchased by Sir Henry Edwards MP. Edwards used this as the basis for acquiring an additional large amount of land in the vicinity.

Edwards began to have the estate developed in 1883 in a rather spread out manner. The various social classes were separated since the most expensive houses were built away from the least expensive.

The station, called Nutfield Station, was opened in 1884 but it is not clear what the relationship was between the railway and the village. It may be significant that Sir Myles Fenton who was General Manager to the South Eastern Railway came to live in the village at that time and that plots of land for houses were sold to Sir Edward Watkin, (also an MP.) who was the Chairman of the SER board. Also Edwards was allowed free travel on the line.

A brick and tile works to the SW of the village (later the acid works, site 187) was purchased by Edwards and its products were used in the construction of the village.

The station at Nutfield (1884) once contained a waiting room, a post office and a ticket office and there was a signal box on the south west side. Sidings served the coal yard to the south west and the adjacent brick works which later became chemical works. The *Station Hotel* was built after 1884 and still stands as a pub. The station master's house stood on the north side

The station died, in the traditional sense, with the steam age in 1967 and since then has been little more than a train stop. The station buildings and the signal were demolished.

The coal sidings were finally built over in 1991-1992.

In preparation for the Channel Tunnel freight traffic a pedestrian over bridge was installed in 1992 to replace the level crossing.

19 GODSTONE STATION
TQ 362 483   ✳

Godstone station has suffered a similar decline to Nutfield station but was once locally important as a centre for distributing coal. Until 1948 there was a coal staging known as Heasman's wharf. (The word 'wharf' has canal connotations.)

The village of South Godstone, which is three miles south of Godstone itself owes its existence to the station

20 RAILWAY ARCH, NUTFIELD
TQ 295 493   ■

The railway bridges the narrow road, Clay Lane, as it approaches Redhill. From the north, Clay Lane dips down steeply to the bridge which is sited on a bend. The railway builders evidently wanted to achieve a great height in the centre of this narrow bridge since it is built in an unusual parabolic shape. It is locally known as the egg arch.

21 THE CATERHAM LINE
TQ 336 590 to TQ 341 554 ■

In the period immediately after 1842 the sole railway line between Croydon and Redhill was shared by the SER and the LBSCR.

The area from Croydon to Caterham and from Croydon to Merstham was very sparsely populated in the mid-nineteenth century and the station on the railway line which served it, Godstone Road, was closed in 1847.

Nevertheless the Caterham Railway was proposed to develop mineral reserves most of which lay to the south of Caterham. These were the stone in the Upper Greensand which was quarried underground on Godstone Hill, chalk and lime, silver sand at Godstone and stone from Tilburstow Hill south of Godstone. Caterham itself provided gravels and brick earth.

The railway was given the Royal Assent in June 1854 and designed to start at the site of the Godstone Road Station (now Purley) of the London, Brighton and South Coast Railway. It offered no great engineering difficulties and when opened in 1856, as a single track, had stations at Kenley, the area we now call Whyteleafe and Caterham.

The Caterham Railway Company failed; partly because the expected revenues from the carriage of minerals did not materialise.

Another reason was that the route to London eventually ran over rails belonging to the London, Brighton and South Coast Railway Company and also to those of the South-Eastern Railway Company.

20: Railway arch, South Nutfield — the Egg Arch
Photo: Chris Shepheard

These two companies were ever in fierce and acrimonious dispute, each fearing that the other would obtain commercial advantage by siding with the Caterham railway. The result was that both hampered the operations of the Caterham railway.

In 1858 a Court case led to the contractor, George Furnace, to whom the Caterham Company could not discharge its debts, being appointed receiver of the Company. In turn, in 1859, the South-Eastern acquired the line.

Despite, at first, offering a poor service the line was to prosper into the twentieth century. This was because bickering about the line between the railway companies ceased and the Caterham Valley rapidly developed as a residential area. George Drew is chiefly associated with this building programme which included houses made from local stone on the main road.

Electrification occurred in 1928

22 WHYTELEAFE SOUTH STATION
TQ 341 578 ✱

When the Caterham railway was built there was only one station in the area of the present village of Whyteleafe which station was first called Warlingham — because at that time Whyteleafe itself did not exist. This station had its name changed to Whyteleafe South in 1956. The station owes its existence solely to the fact that the Caterham Railway Act required that a station or lodge be built where the railway crossed the road on the level.

Whyteleafe South (Warlingham) station was rebuilt in 1862 but 'Station House', 1857, still remains. Its front door is bricked up and has a piece of South-Eastern type awning over it. With a wooden seat under it, it looks like a shrine to the SER.

The road (now very deteriorated), 'The Avenue' at the station was built by the railway company as a carriage road for George Padbury, JP who was the owner of the estate in this locality. It was part of the bargaining process and led to now vanished Manor Cottage.

23 WHYTELEAFE STATION
TQ 338 585 ✱

Work on improving the Caterham line started in 1897 and was completed by 1 January 1900. The improvements were to double the track, open a new Station at Whyteleafe (Whyteleafe Station) and replace the station at Caterham with a larger one.

24 THE SURREY AND SUSSEX JUNCTION RAILWAY
TQ 337 593 to TQ 424 483 ■

Before 1884 London and Brighton were connected solely by the London Brighton and South Coast's line through Redhill. Plans by the South Eastern Company, in 1863, to construct an alternative line to Brighton and also to Eastbourne were successfully opposed by the Brighton Company. Retaliatory plans by the Brighton Company to back independent companies to construct lines from East Grinstead to Groombridge and Croydon to Groombridge were, or the other hand, successful. The company formed to build the latter line was called the Surrey and Sussex Junction Railway Company and work started in 1865 under the contractors Messrs. Waring.

The work ceased in 1869 which was a time of financial stringency heralded by the financial collapse of London's biggest discount bank Overend Gurney and Co. 10 May 1866.

Also the SER argued vehemently that the railway violated an agreement of 1864, which constrained the LBSCR from building in this area, and eventually, the Duke of Richmond was asked to arbitrate. As a result (1869) ownership of the S & SJR was transferred to the LBSCR. who were subject to penalties if they failed to complete it. Nevertheless despite a fine of £32,250 the Brighton Company did abandon the project.

25 MARDEN PARK VIADUCT
TQ 353 570 ■

This five-arched brick viaduct near Marden Park was built in the time of the Surrey and Sussex Junction Railway.

There is a cottage at the foot of the viaduct on the north-east side of the road which looks like former railway property and is named Viaduct Cottage.

26 STAFFHURST WOOD
TQ 412 485 ✱

The English navvies working on the Surrey and Sussex Junction Railway in 1865-9 demanded too high wages and Belgians were brought in. It is believed some were camped at Staffhurst Wood. The Belgians got a scandalously poor deal. Apart from being attacked by rioting English navvies at Mark Beech in Kent, they suffered and died from accident, smallpox and cholera.

27 LIMPSFIELD CHURCHYARD
TQ 405 532 ✱

The grave of Harriet Kennard in Saint Peter's Churchyard, Limpsfield is of a lady who died of cholera after nursing the sick Belgium railway navvies at Staffhurst Wood.

28 THE OXTED LINE
TQ 337 593 to TQ 395 395 ■

In 1877 companies, independent of the two major companies competing in the area, obtained acts allowing the construction of lines from Lewes to East Grinstead and from Haywards Heath to East Grinstead. In 1878 the Brighton Company obtained powers to connect East Grinstead to Croydon. From Croydon to Oxted the line followed the old S&SJ Railway. Joseph Firbank was the contractor for all these works.

The completion of Oxted Tunnel, the stations, the lattice girder bridges and the branch lines to the chalk pits and brick works date to Firbank's time and later.

29 OXTED TUNNEL
TQ 365 554 to TQ 377 539 ■

Oxted tunnel is 2087 metres long, curves, and was dug by sinking shafts along its length from the surface at intervals of 200 yards. The shafts were sunk in the time of the Surrey and Sussex Junction Railway (1865-7) but the tunnel was completed by Joseph Firbank between 1878-84. It was the longest tunnel built by Firbank and heavy springs were encountered at the base of the chalk. (There was a roof fall on 15 June 1917.) The tunnel slopes downwards to the south, and therefore discharges a significant quantity of River Wandle catchment basin water out into the catchment area of the Eden.

30 UPPER WARLINGHAM STATION
TQ 342 583 ✱

Upper Warlingham (Upper Warlingham and Whyteleafe from 1894 to 1900) was a substantial station with coal sidings (Up and Down sides) and sidings to a chalk pit. By 1968 most of these had been removed.

31 WOLDINGHAM STATION
TQ 359 564 ✱

Woldingham station was opened as Marden Park and a siding may be left in place for a motorised trolley employed on tunnel maintenance.

32 OXTED STATION
TQ 393 527 ✱

Extensive coal and delivery sidings were removed from the up side in 1969.

33 LINGFIELD BRICKWORKS (SOMETIMES CALLED CROWHURST BRICKWORKS)

TQ 394 464 ■

The siding to Lingfield brick works closed in the 1950s when the works changed from coal to oil. Its original purpose was to bring coal to the works and take bricks from the works. It was also used to bring in garbage for tipping in old pits.

34 LINGFIELD STATION

TQ 394 438 ✳

Lingfield station was once of great importance as a race course station. Race traffic emanated from both London and Brighton. After WWII banana ripening sheds were set up in the sidings at the up end. Trains of refrigerated

34: *above:* The Oxted line passing through Lingfield station; *below:* Banana ripening sheds at Lingfield station   *Photos: Chris Shepheard*

vans carried the traffic. The trade has ceased but the sheds remain

34: *below:* Lingfield station from the front
Photo: Chris Shepheard

35 OXTED LIMEWORKS SIDING

TQ 383 536

This siding was opened in 1886

There was an exchange siding beside the main line and the two short wagon roads. A cutting curved right handed up to the works. Here there were sidings served by the two-foot gauge railway which went into the pit. The branch ceased about 1939 and the rails were lifted in 1969.

36 OXTED VIADUCT

TQ 395 525 ■

At Oxted, Cooks Pond and Riddlesdown chalk-pit wrought-iron lattice girder viaducts were constructed utilising elegant brick piers. It is likely that some of the brickwork was started in the time of the S&S Junction Railway.

37 COOKS POND VIADUCT

TQ 398 402 ■

The lattice girder bridge at Cooks Pond is of five spans of 125ft and is 65ft above the rail track. No one knows the origin of the Cooks Pond which is a very picturesque stretch of water.

38 CROWHURST JUNCTION

TQ 400 480

The 1878 railway line between East Grinstead and Croydon was to be jointly owned by the LBSCR and the SER between South Croydon and Crowhurst Junction North. Here a spur line was to join the SER Redhill to Tonbridge line.

South of the junction the railway was to be entirely LBSCR property.

The junction was opened on 10 March 1884 and lasted until 10 June 1955 when it passed out of scheduled use. Later following the removal of the points it ceased to be of any use. The embankments still remain and are visible from the train.

39 HURST GREEN JUNCTION

TQ 401 511

On 3 January 1888 the Oxted and Groom-bridge line was opened from Hurst Green junction. It was started in 1885 after an Act of 1881. As the senior Joseph Firbank died in 1886 it was completed by his eldest son Joseph T Firbank.

40 HURST GREEN STATION

TQ 400 514 *

Hurst Green Station was formerly a wooden structure opened on the south side of the road on 1 June 1907. It was re-sited and built in brick and became a station rather than a halt on 12 June 1961.

36: Oxted railway viaduct

Photo: Chris Shepheard

The eighteenth century entrepreneurs perceive the Downs and The Weald of Surrey and Sussex as inaccessible sparsely populated tracts of wilderness where the people were impoverished and demoralised. The root cause of the problem was the parlous state of the roads which severely inhibited trade and social connections with London. Proposed answers were to penetrate these counties in the first place with canals and later with railways. By these means it was thought that industrialisation could be encouraged by bringing cheap coal. Part of the industrialisation would be the exploitation of the mineral reserves such as chalk, sand, fuller's earth, stone, clay and iron ore. Agriculture would also be improved, as from chalk lime could be manufactured in large quantities. Lime was regarded as an essential manure for the improvement of agricultural land.

A further reason for developing canals and railway lines across the region was to connect London with ports such as Portsmouth on the south coast. Without overland routes for transportation Portsmouth was linked to London only by sailing vessels which were forced to brave the storms of the English Channel and the Straits of Dover. In times of war enemy action was a danger and even in peace piracy could occur.

The chief obstacle to the canal and railway builders, as far as reaching The Weald was concerned, was the North Downs. Thus the Croydon, Merstham and Godstone extension of the Surrey Iron Railway (which was a horse tramway) reached only the southern foot of the North Downs although it had found its way to the Merstham gap without tunnelling. Further extension into the Weald would have meant cutting through the Upper Greensand ridge through what we now know as Rockshaw Road. The CMGIR's Act empowered an extension of the 'main line' to Reigate and a collateral branch to Godstone but these never came into being.

CANAL SCHEMES

There were at least two schemes for canal building using the Merstham gap. The first by John Rennie, 1803, proposed a long tunnel between Coulsdon and Merstham. It would have connected the Croydon Canal with Portsmouth. Edward Banks' plan, 1810, was dependent on a different scheme which was to construct the Grand Southern Canal across the south of England. He proposed to take a branch off it at Copthorne and connect it with the Croydon, Merstham and Godstone extension of the Surrey Iron Railway at Quarry Dean. The only tunnel needed would have been under Rockshaw Road.

These canal schemes had in common that they would have passed through the marshes in the north of Nutfield Parish and through the marshy area we now know as Redhill. From thence The Weald could be reached by following the brook which meanders through Earlswood dodging the hills of the Lower Greensand.

41 CANAL COTTAGE, NUTFIELD MARSH

TQ 302 514 ■

But it was all too near the railway age and the canal schemes never came to fruition. Canal Cottage on Nutfield Marsh has a name which stands as a reminder to these schemes but it was actually built in the late 17th century though modified later.

19 HEASMAN'S WHARF, GODSTONE STATION

TQ 362 483 ■

Until the 1950s another structure with canal connotations was Heasman's Wharf at Godstone Station which was a coal staging. The navigation of the partially canalised upper Medway at Tonbridge was in the coal business and the opening of the railway from Tonbridge to Redhill in 1842 offered them the opportunity of transporting coal from Tonbridge for sale at Godstone. This occurred despite the SER's initial lack of cooperation.

The partially canalised upper Medway played a key role in the construction of the railway line between Tonbridge and Redhill. It was laid from the Tonbridge end with rails brought up the Medway. And it is of note that the inhabitants of Tonbridge were very impatient for a railway even at this very early stage of the railway age.

42: Redhill aerodrome   *Photo: Chris Shepheard*

42 REDHILL AERODROME, SOUTH NUTFIELD

TQ 300 480   ■

This aerodrome started in 1934 when British Air Transport left Croydon Airport. Graham Douglas became Managing Director and the company bought Ham Farm. H Edwards and A A Douglas were also directors.

It was A G Douglas who founded Redhill Flying Club in 1937.

In 1938 the Civil Air Guard was formed. This was a scheme by which men and women could learn to fly at subsidised fees (12.5p per hour) provided they undertook to serve in the RAF in times of emergency. The CAG hut stills stand inside the aerodrome gate.

Six new hangars were built in 1938 to accommodate extra aircraft which were needed because British Air Transport were training Volunteer Reservists.

During the war the aerodrome became a satellite airfield for Kenley fighter station.

During 1941-42 the perimeter track was laid and blister hangars, concrete air-craft stands and aircrew huts were dispersed along it. The stream was culverted and a bombproof battle headquarters (underground) was constructed to the south of Hale Farm.

An important war-time function of the airfield was to be a satellite fighter station to Kenley but Balloon Barrage Command occupied the site later in the war until May 1945. After this it was used as a very large ammunition dump which was not cleared until 1947.

In September 1944, wounded from the Arnhem airborne assault were flown in to be transferred to the Smallfield Hospital.

After the war the airfield was once again used for private flying, principally by the Tiger Club, but this ceased about 1990 and the future of the site became uncertain. It became locally feared that a concrete runway would be constructed allowing small jet planes to land and the site to become an adjunct to Gatwick.

Other activities which sprang up after the war include the establishment of an engineering firm; of helicopter firms of which Bristow's was the most important, and of Brake Brothers–a food firm utilising some of the former spacious hangers for storage. This last firm took over their premises from the MOD who previously garaged 'Green Goddess' fire appliances for use by the Civil Defence.

There was also an aeronautics school until the 1950s

An unusual enterprise which started before WWII was the grass drying plant. This utilised the grass mowings from the airfield itself.

43 KENLEY AERODROME

TQ 328 758   ■

This Aerodrome was started with part of Kenley Common being compulsorily acquired under the Defence of the Realm Act (DORA) in 1917 despite public protest. It was first used as an Aeroplane Acceptance Park. Aeroplane parts were delivered in crates from the nearby stations and the planes assembled and tested before delivery for immediate wartime service in France. It was not used to defend London against German bombers (Gothas) and Zeppelins during this WWI period.

Modernisation was effected under the Whyteleafe building and civil engineering contractor, J B Edwards between 1931 and 1934. This established Kenley as a permanent fighter station. Concrete runways were laid in 1939 and were ready for the Battle of Britain in 1940.

Its crucial role in the defence of Britain during WWII was as HQ B sector in No II fighter group which covered the area from London to Shoreham and London to Pevensey.

It was severely damaged on 18 August 1940 by a force of low flying German Dorniers and Junkers Ju88 dive bombers but this had little military significance. Afterwards the vulnerable sector operations building (demolished 1980) was vacated and its function transferred on 3 September 1940 to Spice and Wallis's empty butcher's premises at 11 Godstone Road, Caterham. This building thereby became one of the most important sites in Britain at the height of the Battle of Britain. It was only used until November 1940 when a more suitable house, The Grange, Old Coulsdon replaced its function. No.11 survived the war, but not later property development, and on its site now stands a modern brick shop; a blue plaque installed by the Bourne Society commemorates its connection with the Battle of Britain.

The aerodrome operated as a fighter station in the following way. A chain of radar stations (Chain Home) on the south coast detected planes over France and the English Channel. Information was passed to the filter room at Stanmore who decided if enemy aircraft were on the way. If so their courses were plotted over England from Royal Observer Posts such as the one on Steners Hill Bletchingley. Kenley would be warned if necessary.

Later in the Battle of Britain the Luftwaffe employed night aircraft against which 219 squadron was supported by 600 squadron night fighters based at Redhill. (No. 600 Squadron was sent north on 14 October 1940 and replaced by No.219 Squadron's own night fighters.) Approaching low flying enemy aircraft would be detected by long-range radar at Pevensey. Control was then passed to a small Ground Controlled Interception radar station at Wartling who could automatically pick out the hostile aircraft with searchlights. British night fighters were directed to the area and were assisted in finding their targets with Air Interception Radar which was installed in each night fighter.

The night fighters were transferred from Redhill to Tangmere in December 1940. It had less foggy weather and concrete runways.

After the war the runways at Kenley were too short for jet fighters and operations were transferred to Biggin Hill.

It was closed in 1959 except for use by the Air Training Corps for gliding. The officers mess was closed in 1974 but was taken over in 1980 by the Home Office. Because it is an area of relatively low electrical interference it had become converted to a Radio Technology Laboratory by 1982 and handed to the Board of Trade.

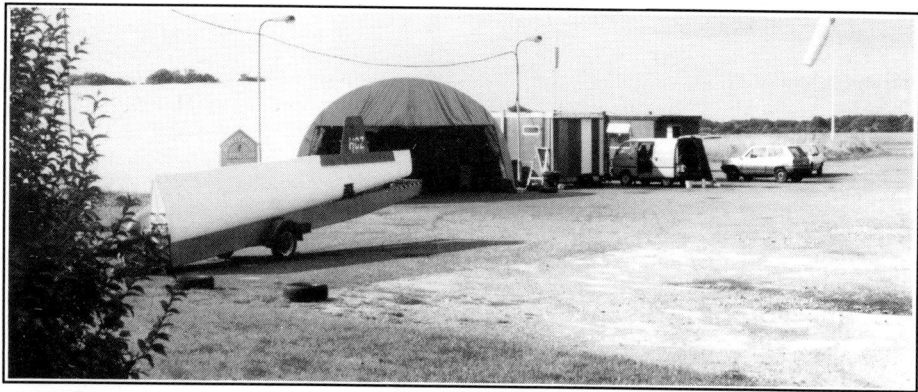

43: Kenley aerodrome

Windmills need to have their sweeps (sails) turned into the wind to work effectively. This is achieved in different ways by two main types of mill.

In post mills the whole structure of the mill is balanced on a post and can normally be turned into the wind by one man operating the tail post at ground level.

The tower mill which is more expensive and more productive, came later and is a tapered structure built on a brick foundation and only the cap on the top, which carries the sweeps, can be revolved for the purpose of turning the sweeps into the wind. Sometimes the cap can be rotated by means of a chain mechanism but more often a fan tail placed diametrically opposite the sweeps automatically directs the cap.

When the body of the tower mill is of timber construction and weatherboarded, such mills are known as smock mills.

Until the nineteenth century windmills served local needs and were sited on ridges and hills. Generally they were post mills and owed their existence to local crops of grain. The Weald being heavily forested, was virtually devoid of windmills.

During the medieval period there is a mention of a windmill at Warlingham (12th century) and at Nutfield (1296).

With the coming of better roads, towards the end of the 18th century, millers aspired to export flour beyond their localities. For this reason windmill sites grew up near the roads on lower ground, and smock mills came into prominence.

The main purpose of windmills in Tandridge District appears to have been to grind corn, more specifically wheat in later times, to provide flour for the baker.

The heyday of the Surrey mills was 1810-1820. By that time farmland had been ploughed to a much greater degree than previously and in fact ploughed to a greater degree than now. The clay soil of the Weald, by now much less forested, and the Gault clay of the Vale of Holmesdale was good for growing grain. The impetus for the industry came from the fact that the Napoleonic wars and the Corn Laws protected the farmers from cheap imports of grain.

In the end it was steam power and eventually cheap and plentiful imports of grain which killed the use of windmills.

It is interesting to reflect, that at the end of the nineteenth century, William Jupp claimed he could count fifteen other windmills from his own mill at Outwood.

44 CATERHAM WINDMILLS

Farries and Mason have identified the sites of two windmills on the high ground at Caterham. Today it would be difficult to locate these sites with exactitude.

WINDMILL I

TQ 329 552

Appears on Rocque's map of 1762 and is said to have been at the southern end of Heath Road and Mill Lane. It had gone by 1736.

WINDMILL 2

TQ 325 563

Dates back to at least 1696 but disappeared during the latter half of the nineteenth century. Its site was just north of a house named 'The Firs' in the northern part of the hospital grounds. During the beginning of the nineteenth century it passed to Richard Dewdney.

45 TILBURSTOW WINDMILL

TQ 354 501

This was a post mill at the summit of Tilburstow Hill south of Godstone and it was a few metres to the east side of the road. Tilburstow Hill is part of the greensand ridge and the mill, which dated from at least 1760, was a very prominent landmark until it collapsed in 1805. There are now no obvious remains

It was another of those mills which were once in the hands of Richard Dewdney of Bletchingley (although owned by Sir Robert Clayton) and therefore it had the alternative name, Dewdney's Mill.

46 GODSTONE GREEN WINDMILL

TQ 348 518

There is a footpath leading north on the west

49: Outwood windmills

side of the Hare and Hounds opposite Godstone Green. The tumulus, which can be seen to the right as the footpath veers diagonally across the field, marks the site of the windmill. Rather shockingly it was built on an ancient barrow.

This mill was the much more conveniently sited replacement for Tilburstow windmill but was still a post mill owned by Sir William Clayton and was worked, at first, by Richard Dewdney until about 1839. It did not survive into the twentieth century but two paintings preserve its memory.

47 LIMPSFIELD CHART WINDMILL
TQ 426 518 ■

This was a post mill situated on the eastward extension of the greensand ridge and built early in the nineteenth century. It was demolished in 1925 but its site is easy to find since it stood between Windmill Cottage and Mill Cottage which is a timber framed house at the junction of Tally Road and Stoneleigh Road. There are photographs of the mill in the nearby Carpenter's Arms.

Information about the mill comes from a bill of sale in 1831, photographs (including one of the demolition), local memory and local records. It seems that until 1876 a steam engine supplemented the wind power. However the most curious fact was that it was a left-handed windmill. Normally the sweeps of a windmill will be seen to rotate in an anti-clockwise direction as viewed facing them. The reason for Limpsfield Chart Windmill doing the opposite is not known.

48 BOTTERY'S WINDMILL, NUTFIELD AND BLETCHINGLEY
TQ 317 507

There is a reference to a windmill in Bletchingley in 1262 and documentary evidence demonstrates one in the field named Woolpits in 1553. From 1736, pictures indicate a post mill. It was another of the picturesque windmills which dominated the skyline on the greensand ridge and was the last of them to be demolished (1929).

Its site straddled the parish boundary between Nutfield and Bletchingley and can be found just south of the A25 and east of the M23. It is on private ground but a Derbyshire peak millstone on the ground is inscribed, **HERE STOOD BOTERYS WINDMILL FROM ABOUT 1300 TO 1929 AD. STOPPED WORKING IN 1888.**

49 OUTWOOD WINDMILL
TQ 328 455   **LSI** ❑

Outwood is founded on a sandstone outcrop in the Weald and the hill so formed affords a good place to site windmills. The post mill still standing there was built in 1665 but it was later joined by a smock mill, built about 1800, probably by William Budgen a miller of Horne. The two together were known as the, 'Cat and Kitten'. The smock mill (the Cat) collapsed in 1960 as a result of its rotten condition.

Outwood smock mill was the largest in England and was the finest of its type in Surrey. The last person to work it seems to have been Edward Scott who transferred from the windmill at Nutfield in 1885. At this time a portable steam engine was brought into use on **15** windless days.

The post mill is now the oldest working windmill in Britain although there are a number of older non-working post mills which have survived. It was working as a commercial milling enterprise until William Jupp, described as the last of the true Surrey millers, died in 1934. It is now worked only as a tourist attraction.

The survival of the post mill and the wealth of accumulated technical information on both of the Outwood mills is the result of the post mill coming into the charge of the Windmill Section of the Society for the Protection of Ancient Buildings.

50 ASHBY'S MILL, WARLINGHAM
TQ 354 585 ■

From their prominent scarp faces, the North Downs slope so gently towards Croydon and the north that a plateau is formed in the Warlingham and Chelsham area. In this highland region windmills have been recorded since the twelfth century. It is a waterless region in which windmills did not have to compete with watermills. Unfortunately the lack of water meant that there was little hope of extinguishing fire, and the mills were in constant danger of being burnt down.

One such mill, burnt down in 1865 was the smock mill, Ashby's Mill, which existed behind the **Leather Bottle** Inn at Warlingham near the present public library. The outbuildings and the Mill House survived until 1948 on the site now occupied by Sheltón Avenue. A fragment of a millstone exhibited in the library's grounds acts as a memorial.

Not far away at the top of Succombs Hill the tithe map of 1844 and other evidence suggests that a windmill once existed here, (**site 51** TQ 350 577).

52 BEADLE'S MILL, CHELSHAM
TQ 367 586 ■

Chelsham Road was formerly Mill Lane and contains Mill House. The post mill which stood 60 yards to the south of its house was burnt down about 1840. Rocque's map indicates that it dated back to at least 1762.

53 HORNE
TQ 333 440

A short distance south of Outwood Mill, down Wilmot's Lane the line of the pill boxes is met. One of them, 300 yards east from Paradise Cottage and a small pond, is the site of a windmill which once existed on the Weald Clay, during the early years of the nineteenth century. Almost nothing is known about this mill.

58: King's Mill, South Nutfield

Roger Packham Collection

The area of Tandridge District south of the North Downs is drained by the river Eden on the east side and the river Mole to the west side. Known watermill sites are mainly on the streams draining into the river Eden.

Watermills broadly divide into two groups. The undershot type and the remaining types which include overshot, breastshot and pitchback.

In the undershot system the water wheel is equipped with paddles and is made to rotate by a fast moving stream hitting the paddles at the bottom of the wheel. This type is not found in Tandridge District. With the exception of an unusual turbine at Oxted, only the overshot type is found in the district. The overshot wheel is equipped with buckets or vanes and the water is applied to the top of the wheel. The weight of the water causes the wheel to rotate and in a direction which is normally away from the pond supplying the water. If it rotates in the opposite direction it is called a pitchback.

The overshot system is a great scenic asset to any district, since overshot wheels require large picturesque mill ponds and high artificial embankments to contain them.

As a general rule the watermills in the Tandridge District were used for corn grinding. Grain, especially wheat in later days, was ground between mill stones to produce flour for the baker. Nevertheless there was a fulling mill at Pendell, gunpowder mills at Leigh mill Godstone, a bone mill at Godstone, a Wealden iron forge mill at Newchapel and rollers were used at the Oxted turbine driven mill instead of stones.

Two types of millstone were in general use. The Derby Grit (Derby Peak, Millstone Grit) was used for grinding barley to produce grist for cattle, whereas the French Burr Stone which ground more finely was used to grind wheat to produce flour for bread.

The roller-mill as built at Oxted produced an even finer flour.

54 COLTSFORD MILL, HURST GREEN

TQ 397 506   **LSII** ❑

Coltsford Mill, a restaurant in 1993, has always, until recently, been a corn mill and is on a small stream which flows down from the high ground at Oxted to the north. It is considered to be on the site of a mill mentioned in the Domesday survey.

The existing buildings are of brick and galletted sandstone to the first floor while the upper two stories to the mansard roof are weatherboarded. Actually the weatherboarding is painted aluminium. Derek Stidder considers that structurally the present buildings date to the mid-18th century. In the sense that it still occasionally grinds corn for private use, it is the only working watermill in Surrey. It ceased working commercially after the second world war.

George Marchant was the miller until 1866 after which William Heasman who came from Rowfant acquired it. The Heasman family continued to own the site until about 1988 and in their early years they worked it in conjunction with Oxted Mill further upstream.

The last miller was Wilfred Heasman.

During the year of his arrival William Heasman installed the present iron waterwheel which now lies hidden below the high embankment.

In the centre of the large mill pond is an unusual, possibly unique basin, with a circumference of 30ft which provides a fast overflow for excess water and obviates the need for a manually operated sluice gate.

55 HAXTED MILL, HAXTED

TQ 419 455   LSII ❑

Haxted Mill, which was a corn mill, is on the river Eden and ceased to be a commercial mill after the Second World War. After this it was purchased in 1949 by Mr Woodrow and thanks to him has become a most interesting working watermill museum which is generally open to the public most days during the summer.

It is built of brick with weatherboarding above the first floor and it is easy to see that the mill is in two parts built at separate times. The western half was built in 1680 on 14th century foundations and the eastern section in 1749. There is nothing to suggest that there was a mill on this site before the 14th century.

Inside, it contains various types of watermill

17

machinery and demonstrates the construction of watermills since the 17th century.

Outside, the cast iron waterwheel is externally mounted on the west wall of the mill but the waterwheel on the roadside comes from a Cornish tin mine.

It was run in conjunction with the Edenbridge Town mill during the 18th and 19th centuries.

56 HEDGECOURT MILL, FELBRIDGE
TQ 360 404 ❏
At the end of Mill Lane north of Copthorne Road
Hedgecourt Pond (42 acres) is one of the largest mill ponds in the south of England. It was built as a pen pond for the wire mill further down the Eden Brook. (See Chapter 7: Wealden iron.)

There was a corn mill on the site in the 16th century but the last mill built dates to the end of the 17th century. It survived into the 20th century but fell into ruin after about 1930. Only traces, including part of the wheel, can now be found. At the turn of the century it was being worked in conjunction with the wire mill. During the middle of the nineteenth century it was worked by L Hardy who also worked the Horne windmill.

It is known to have had an iron overshot waterwheel and a pen and ink drawing of the 1920s shows it was of stone construction to the first floor and then weatherboarded.

The Miller's cottage remains at the site — enlarged and modernised.

57 IVY MILL, GODSTONE
TQ 348 511 ■
Ivy Mill was a substantial building on a brook called Lower Dill, which feeds Stratton Brook then Gibbs Brook and thence the river Eden. Its site is to be found in Ivy Mill Lane, not far from Godstone Green.

Always a corn mill, its name derives from Ivy House. This was because in the seventeenth century the Manor of Stangrave in which the mill stood passed to the Northey family who built Ivy House. Ivy House is now called Stangrave Hall and stands on the A25 north west of the mill.

A mill, Chevington, mentioned in the Domesday survey probably stood on the site. Stangrave estate eventually passed to the Clayton family and the mill remained in their possession until purchased by Sir William Greenwell in 1907.

18 The mill as existing in the 20th century was brick-built but was destroyed by fire in 1924

two years after it stopped working.

Today it is easy to discern where the millpond was, and traces of brickwork at the former sluice gates still remain. The mill house, Ivy Mill House built by Charles Ridley in 1698, still stands on the site.

The very modernised dwelling named The Barn was, at the beginning of the century, stables for the horses involved in cartage of the flour to places such as Caterham where about 1900 Mr Bromley Hall, who lived in Ivy Mill Cottage and owned the mill, had a corn-chandler's business .

58 KING'S MILL, SOUTH NUTFIELD
TQ 299 489 ■
In King's Mill Lane
This is a small weatherboarded mill and, in 1992, stood well preserved as office accommodation. It was built before 1768 as evidenced by John Rocque's map of that year. It ceased to be a water powered mill in 1944 but corn milling continued by electricity until 1963. The pond has now been filled and the river diverted from the mill site. The engineering works adjoining it dates from the 1960s. In its day it must have presented an interesting sight since the external iron waterwheel was greater in width (11 feet) than in diameter (9 feet). At one time there was a Cornish boiler and steam engine on site.

The water mill mentioned for the locality in the Domesday survey is not likely to be the one on the King's Mill site. However it is possible that there was once an earlier mill somewhere near Hale Farm at a site now grassed over by Redhill aerodrome.

59 LEIGH MILL, GODSTONE
TQ 362 509 LSII ■
Leigh Mill is at Leigh Place on Gibb's Brook and is set in a picturesque and complex area of lakes, streams, woodlands and hills. Now a private residence near Leigh Place.

It was not mentioned in the Domesday survey but was in use during the 14th century and by the end of the 16th century gunpowder was being manufactured under the direction of George Evelyn. However in 1635 Charles I appointed Samuel Cordwell and George Collins of the Chilworth gunpowder mills near Guildford as his gunpowder makers. As a result Leigh Mill reverted to corn milling. Milling ceased in 1934.

The mill is now a private residence and it is possible, with a little difficulty, to see the slowly

61: Oxted Mill

Photo: Chris Shepheard

deteriorating iron waterwheel while standing on the dam, which is a public footpath, on the north west side of the former mill building.

60 NUTFIELD MILL

TQ 307 499 ■

John Rocque's map of 1768 names the hamlet at the present Mid Street in South Nutfield as Mill Street. This coupled to the discovery of documents by Mr Richard Deacon of South Nutfield referring to a water mill at Little Cormonger's farm during the 17th century seems to indicate a water mill at this site. There is a small pond still in existence fed by springs but no other sign of a mill. The site is on the hill side and the stream issuing from it has been piped away.

Is this Nutfield's Domesday mill site?

61 OXTED MILL, OXTED

TQ 390 518   **LSII** ■

In Spring Lane. South west of the High Street

This has been a water mill site since the mid-19th century but a second mill was built as an extension to the first in 1893. Both mill buildings are of red brick but the newer one is in the style of a Victorian warehouse.

It is possible to descend to the stream bed at the back of the mill and look under the buildings. Here can be seen the rusting remains of the old iron waterwheel, enclosed when the later mill was built, and a later rare

Girard turbine which powered the 1893 mill.

The mill of 1893 was a roller mill and was built at the time that William Heasman, also of Coltsford Mill, was the miller. Powered by the turbine it gave a finer grade flour than the older mill but consumed far more water to grind the same quantity of wheat. Thus Coltsford Mill farther down stream was worked at the same time as the turbine was used because this was its time of maximum water supply.

Small crude wooden plaques from the mill are on exhibit (1993) at Joyces-on-the-Chart which is the restored village bakery, now a teashop and restaurant, situated at the Village shop Limpsfield Chart. The plaques, Heasman family heirlooms, read:

THIS NEW MILL WAS BUILT 1892-1895. Geo. WORSSELL, CARPENTER, OXTED. F SALES, BRICKLAYER, OXTED, Wal SHOVE, BRICK-LAYER, OXTED. FIRST STARTED TO GRIND WITH MACHINERY 19th JUNE 1893, 21 MINUTES PAST 3 PM.

BINS BUILT DECEMBER 1893, Geo WORSSALL DECEMBER 8th 1893, Mr. AND Mrs HEASMAN, CAROLINE HEASMAN, DAUGHTER; FLORANCE HEASMAN, DAUGHTER; HILTON HEASMAN SON, ALL ILL WITH INFLUENZA. SIGNED Geo WORSSELL.

19

65: Wire Mill, Newchapel   *Photo: Chris Shepheard*

Flour milling ceased in 1951 and the buildings still find use as small business accommodation.

Apart from the mill buildings, still present to admire is the mill pond and waterways, the early 18th century mill cottage and six millstones leaning against the side of the mills at the road side. These stones miraculously seem to avoid the attention of vandals and four of them are French burr millstones.

62 OXTED UPPER MILL, OXTED

TQ 387 523

In High Street

Senex's map of 1729 shows a mill at a site on the stream behind the present *Wheatsheaf* public house. There is no trace of it now.

63 PENDELL MILL, SITE AT MILL COTTAGE

TQ 312 517   ■

One can stand on the dam serving a former water mill, above and on the east side of Mill Cottage. The remnants of the mill pond are just discernible but are largely beneath the M23 and the large artificial hill, known as 'the bund' which is on the east side of the M23.

The bund came into being when the owner of Pendell House rented its ground for tipping in the late 1980s. It was completed by 1991.

The nearby Lakes Farm presumably owes its name partly to the mill pond.

Derek Moore, the owner of Mill Cottage (1991) holds information on the mill.

64 WARE MILL, LINGFIELD

TQ 395 423

The construction of Lingfield Park Racecourse necessitated the destruction of Ware Mill and its pond. Little is known about this mill on this tributary to the river Medway except that it was a nineteenth century cornmill. Today it is remembered by Old Mill house and Mill Wood.

65 WIRE MILL, NEWCHAPEL

TQ 368 418   ✱

On the Eden Brook on a turning off the A22

In 1788 this mill was described as a wire mill. Wire mill operated a forge for the Wealden iron industry in the Middle Ages (See Chapter 7: Wealden Iron). The site was known as Woodcock Hammer until 1823 at which time a corn mill was built. It closed down in 1912 and after being used by a fishing club it was converted to a hotel in 1934 and a country club in 1962 but in 1993 was a popular pub and restaurant.

The mill building is of brick and weatherboarding, no waterwheel or machinery is extant but the pond makes the site very attractive.

7   WEALDEN IRON

Iron was produced in the Wealden area of Surrey, Sussex and Kent since before Roman times and continued until the early part of the nineteenth century. The most productive period was the 16th century when the bloomery furnace gave way to the blast furnace and it also became possible to cast iron cannon. After the 16th century, for various reasons, the industry began to decline. Abraham Darby I's discovery, in 1709 at Coalbrookdale, that coal could replace charcoal as the reducing agent for the smelting of iron ore, eventually resulted in coal districts well away from the Weald becoming paramount in iron production. The Wealden iron industry, once the most important in Britain, became extinct during the early years of the nineteenth century.

Tandridge District was on the periphery of the Wealden iron industry but despite this there is archaeological and documentary evidence for bloomeries and a forge associated with a blast furnace. It should be noted that not only was Wealden clay iron ore, which was dug from pits, essential for the iron production but so also were expanses of coppiced woodland to provide the charcoal. Clay itself was also necessary for furnace building.

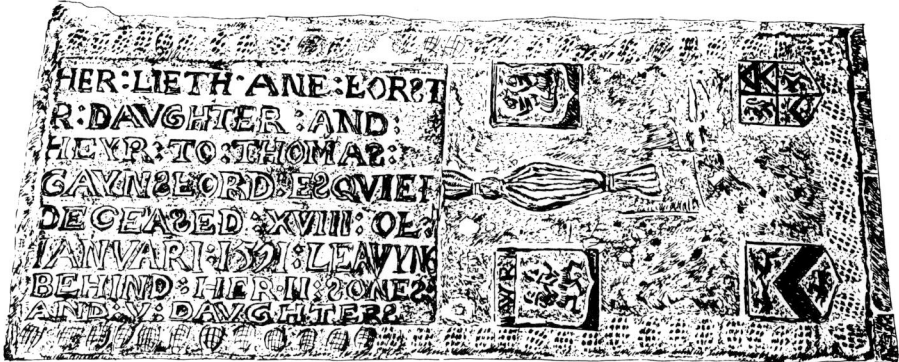

71: Wealden iron grave slab at St George's Church, Crowhurst

Drawing by Peter Watkins

66 CINDERHILL WOOD, SOUTH PARK, BLETCHINGLEY

TQ 337 485.

This is the site, in the Weald clay, of the most northerly bloomery yet found.

Bloomery furnaces were simply layers of iron ore and charcoal heaped into a dome and enclosed with clay. Temperatures high enough to reduce the ore were obtained by the manual use of bellows at the bottom of the furnace. A hole at the top allowed gases to escape. A semi-solid 'bloom' of very impure iron was produced which was separated from the liquid slag. The slag contained iron but removed the silicon impurity in the ore by chemical combination. The bloom needed reheating and hammering to free it of residual slag and produce malleable wrought iron of an acceptable level of purity.

This site, as with numerous other Wealden iron sites was identified by the copious amounts of the clinkery mass, known as cinder, which the iron making processes produced.

67 POUNDHILL, SOUTH PARK, BLETCHINGLEY

TQ 328 483

This site next to Cinderhill recalls the pounding or hammering of the unworked blooms to produce the malleable iron.

68 CINDERHILL, BLINDLEY HEATH

TQ 359 458

Ernest Straker considered that traces of cinder and a pit indicate the presence of an ancient bloomery at this spot.

69 WIRE MILL LAKE, FELBRIDGE

TQ 367 416

The Romans introduced the shaft bloomery furnace which was a drum shaped structure and larger than the dome-type. Its advantage was that ore and charcoal could be added through a hole in the top even while the furnace was being fired. The blast furnace carried this adaptation further. It was larger, constructed of sandstone blocks lined with clay, and by using water power to operate the bellows, molten iron, which could be tapped off, was produced.

No blast furnaces are known to exist in the Tandridge District the nearest one being Warren Furnace just over the border on the Eden Brook near Crawley Down, TQ 348 393. Blast furnaces produced brittle cast or pig iron. To produce the malleable iron required by the blacksmith the carbon had to be burned out by re-melting pig iron in an open charcoal-fired hearth (the finery) and subjecting it to an oxidising air blast. This produced a bloom (and much slag) which required further purification by hammering. Finally, using a second hearth, the chafery, the iron was heated and hammered into a bar. These processes were water-powered and Wire Mill Lake provided the water for Woodcock Hammer or Woodcock Forge which was the former name of the site.

Woodcock Hammer or Woodcock Forge owes its existence to Warren Furnace and in 1574 was worked by John Thorpe. But the furnace fell into disuse only to be rebuilt in a local revival of the Wealden iron industry (against the general trend) during the 1760s. However by 1787 the furnace was abandoned. The forge was certainly in use from 1758 to 1774 and Ernest Straker said '. . . By tradition, nails for St. Paul's Cathedral were made here . . . .'

By 1788 the forge is described as a wire mill but by 1862 it had become a flour mill. A fishing club and hotel had become established on the site by 1934 and eventually the mill became a popular large pub. (See also Water Mills: Site 65)

70 HEDGECOURT LAKE, FELBRIDGE
TQ 360 404 ■

This large popular and attractive lake lies upstream of Wire Mill Lake on the Eden Brook and it was a pen-pond for Woodcock Hammer. That is to say it acted as a reservoir of water.

71 ST. GEORGE'S CHURCH, CROWHURST
TQ 391 474 ✳

The products for which the Wealden iron industry is chiefly remembered are, cannon, fire-backs and graveslabs. The only Wealden iron graveslab in Surrey (1591) is set in the floor of St. George's church, close to the altar, and preserves the memory of the Gaynesford family. It was used as a pattern for fire-backs.

---

8 OPEN PITS

North east Surrey has long been noted for its open pits. Those relating to the extraction of fuller's earth, brick earth, clay, Wealden iron and chalk are mentioned under other headings.

SAND EXTRACTION

Extraction of sand from the Lower Greensand has been a very extensive industry in Tandridge District. It is principally the Folkestone Beds which have been dug. Even within this stratum there is variation in the quality of the sand, there being a coarser yellow iron stained sand, used for building, and a finer white sand known as silica or silver sand which is used for glass making, for moulding sand and for other special purposes.

Sand extraction was still in progress in 1993 and the sand is transported to Hepworth's works on the Holmthorpe estate in Merstham for processing and distribution.

It is unfortunate that there seems to have been no research into the history of this large industry.

72–73 SILICA SAND PIT, NORTH PARK, GODSTONE
TQ 335 519 ■

This is a very modern pit which was still being worked in 1993. The face is at the west end and has been worked for some years by earth movers for the almost white silica sand. This has caused the pit to expand westward but it has been landscaped behind it and no serious environmental damage has occurred.

22 The sand is conveyed by conveyer belt to a very large hopper (**site 73**, TQ 342 517) on the east side of the lane leading from the A25 to North Park Farm. The hopper feeds lorries which take the sand to Merstham.

74 WORKING SAND PIT, BLETCHINGLEY
TQ 307 524 ■

A sand pit was opened on this site in 1990-1991. When observed it was worked by one digger and two lorries. The sand was conveyed to the Holmthorpe works in Merstham by a conveyer belt which was fed from a hopper at the pit.

78: Landfill site at Godstone

Photo: Chris Shepheard

75 76 77 78 79 LANDFILL SITES

Since the 1970s disused sand pits have been utilised as landfill sites. Although this has the benefit of restoring land to agricultural or amenity usage, on the debit side there is the loss of certain landscape features which have become interesting over the years and also the destruction of the wild-life which has colonised these pits. It is regrettable that in Tandridge District we will soon have no example left of the vertical sand cliff faces which exemplify former quarrying methods.

Filled sites are at

TQ 313 522 (Site 75), TQ 374 523 (Site 76)
TQ 332 502 (Site 77)

In 1993 sites being filled were the East Surrey Water Company's reservoir (also a nature reserve) behind Godstone at

TQ 345 518 (Site 78)

and the landscaped area (Fairall's pit) which backs onto Godstone High Street at

TQ 349 520 (Site 79)

The reservoir was being filled, by the water company, with inert material. The adjacent reservoir, (**site 80**, TQ 347 520), was as yet undisturbed and was by now a rare example of a steep sided sand pit still extant in the district.

GRAVEL PITS

Hoggin which consists of small stones in a clay matrix is extracted near Chelsham. It is used for the foundations of drives since it is easy to roll down and provides a durable surface.

81 BROOMFIELD EAST QUARRY

TQ 387 581 ∎

This was opened by Dougal Ballast Co Ltd in 1992. One of the projects at that time was supplying the M25 motorway service station

then under construction at Clacket's Lane

82 BROOMBANK QUARRY

TQ 384 580 ∎

This is a worked-out hoggin pit.

STONE PITS.

Stone was mainly extracted from the Hythe beds of the Lower Greensand at and near Limpsfield Chart.

Quarries are recorded in the Doomesday book and provided grey stone for local houses. The stone when first quarried is yellow or golden brown. It weathers to a greenish grey colour. It is not easy to chisel and was shaped with axes.

Chert, also dug in the vicinity of Limpsfield was mainly used for road building.

A very dark and hard ironstone, known as carstone, is also used in buildings but chiefly around Limpsfield. It was collected from the Folkestone beds of the Lower Greensand and is set in buildings with its bedding planes vertical.

83 CHERT PITS near ST. ANDREW'S CHURCH, LIMPSFIELD CHART

TQ 429 517 ✳

Traces of these former pits may be detected

on the south side of the B269 and east of the church.

23

84 STONE PIT AT RABIES HEATH ROAD, TILBURSTOW HILL

TQ 345 502

This former pit in the Hythe Beds was worked for chert for use in road metalling at the beginning of the century. It is now a nature reserve.

85 PALUDINA LIMESTONE PIT

TQ 341 489

A very thin seam of this shelly limestone outcrops in the Weald Clay. It is a shelly limestone which can be polished and has therefore acquired the name, Surrey Marble. Examples of this, taken from a small pit and incorporated into buildings may be found at South Park Farm, Bletchingley.

86 COB HILL

TQ 359 534

In the dell near Cob Hill mine, which is below Marden Park Lodge, hearthstone was extracted, to a limited extent, opencast. (See Site 102: Cob Hill mine.)

9   FULLERS EARTH PITS

DEFINITION AND USAGE

Fuller's earth is found in the Sandgate beds which lie on the ridge of the Lower Greensand which between Redhill and Bletchingley constitutes the A25. It is a non-plastic clay which will break up into a powder in excess water. Its complex chemical properties imparts to it the power of absorbing large quantities of grease which means that, in the past, newly woven woollen cloth when worked in a mixture of fuller's earth and water was degreased and dirt removed. This is the process of scouring. The process by which the yarn of the cloth was drawn tightly together to form a more wind resistant cloth was the actual fulling or felting process. Confusingly it is not clear what part, if any, fuller's earth played in the actual fulling process.

The use of fuller's earth in cloth manufacture largely died in the nineteenth century but various other often ingenious and very profitable uses were found for it.

The decolorisation and deodorisation of vegetable oils and other edible oils, was a process important in the newly emerged margarine industry at the end of last century. Fuller's earth proved to be an effective agent for this purpose. Especially useful in this context was the fact that in the 1920s a more powerful form of the earth, 'activated fuller's earth' was invented by treating fuller's earth, as dug, with acid. In east Surrey it was convenient that sulphuric acid was available from the nearby Nutfield Chemical Works.

Later an important use became the refinement of lubricating oils. In its role in refining oils, fuller's earth is called a bleaching earth.

Another use in the oil industry was to act as a catalyst to modify certain chemical processes. The earth has also found to be important in catalytic reactions outside the oil industry.

A completely different use was to mix the earth with foundry sands as a bonding agent. This opened up a large sales market.

By treating fuller's earth with soda solution, bentonite is formed. This can be formulated to form a thixotropic suspension and has therefore formed the basis of non-drip paints.

Bentonite is also used as a drilling mud in the oil industry. While agitated by a rotating drill bit it becomes a lubricant. Otherwise it helps to stabilise the drill hole.

Another use of bentonite is as a swelling earth. If it is incorporated into diaphragm walls it will form a water-impervious barrier. This is because in contact with water, bentonite swells and blocks the passage of any further water.

EXTRACTION

The extraction of fuller's earth in Surrey is first mentioned in 1577 but it is likely that pits were well established by that time. It is believed that the original method of extraction was to sink shafts through up to 40 feet of overburden and dig chambers when the fuller's earth stratum was reached (Bell pits). These early pits, it is believed, were mostly dug in the area of Redstone Hill.

In the nineteenth century large open pits came into being.

It is likely that the earth was first sold by farmers but the first person to devote his business life solely to the extraction of the fuller's earth was William Grece near the end of the 18th century.

In the late 1840s James Cawley, formerly of Bletchingley started the development of the area west of Nutfield Village and on the north side of the present A25 which acquired the name of Cockley works. For most of the 20th century this was to become a dominating feature of the landscape and provide a highly industrialised vista.

Almost at the same time Park Works was opened on the north side of Nutfield village

In 1890 a cartel, the Fuller's Earth Union, was formed by amalgamating the companies working the east Surrey pits with those working the Somerset pits.

The era of fuller's earth and its associated pits and works in east Surrey was drawing to a close in 1993. The Fuller's Earth Union was merged with Laporte in 1954 and in 1981 processing activities were transferred to Widnes. The pits in Surrey continued to be worked but the only plant work which was retained was to crush, dry and screen the excavated earth. This produced 'cat litter', or if higher drying temperatures are used, dustless granules. In agriculture these can be used to apply toxic pesticides (adsorbed into the granules) without producing a toxic dust.

Fuller's earth is still a most important mineral but the Surrey pits are now exhausted and planning permission was refused (1990-1992) to exploit the remaining local reserves.

87 COPYHOLD WORKS

TQ 288 502 On north side of the A25.

Just outside the Tandridge District

In 1993 this was the last surviving fuller's earth plant and was used for crushing, drying and screening the earth. It was unlikely to survive much longer than 1994.

The great pits to the north of it which merge into sand pits were at the point of exhaustion and in 1993 are largely operated as landfill sites.

88 CHART LODGE

TQ 289 501 ■

On south side of the A25

This house (1780) was built by John William Grece who was the first person to devote his whole business life to fuller's earth. Behind it and to the west is interesting worked ground which is the remains of Grece's Chartfield pit dating to the early years of the 19th century.

89 GREEN HUT, FULLERS WOOD LANE

TQ 295 503 ■

At east corner of junction of Fullers Wood Lane and the A25

The hut contains an electrical transformer but it was discovered in 1982 that it was the site of vestiges of underground workings. Only a small proportion of fuller's earth was ever mined underground in east Surrey but from time to time underground galleries have been uncovered by later working.

A more spectacular demonstration of underground workings was a nearby collapse of the A25 in 1962.

90 PARK WORKS, NUTFIELD

TQ 305 507 ■

At end of Blacklands Meadow

Park works was a collection of substantial brick buildings from the nineteenth century and constituted a processing plant. It was demolished in 1988. The cleared site which is behind the old village school on the north side of the A25 in Nutfield village was clearly discernable in 1993.

Park works was probably built for James Cawley who came from Bletchingley. He was the man who started a large development of pits in the area between Park works and Cormongers Lane later to be called Cockley Quarry.

91 COCKLEY WORKS

TQ 298 507 ■

Large pits were worked here for over 100 years into the 1980s but the plant was stripped out in 1981 and finally demolished in 1988. The pits were then used for land filling which was completed in 1993 and the site landscaped.

88: Chart Lodge   *Photo: Chris Shepheard*

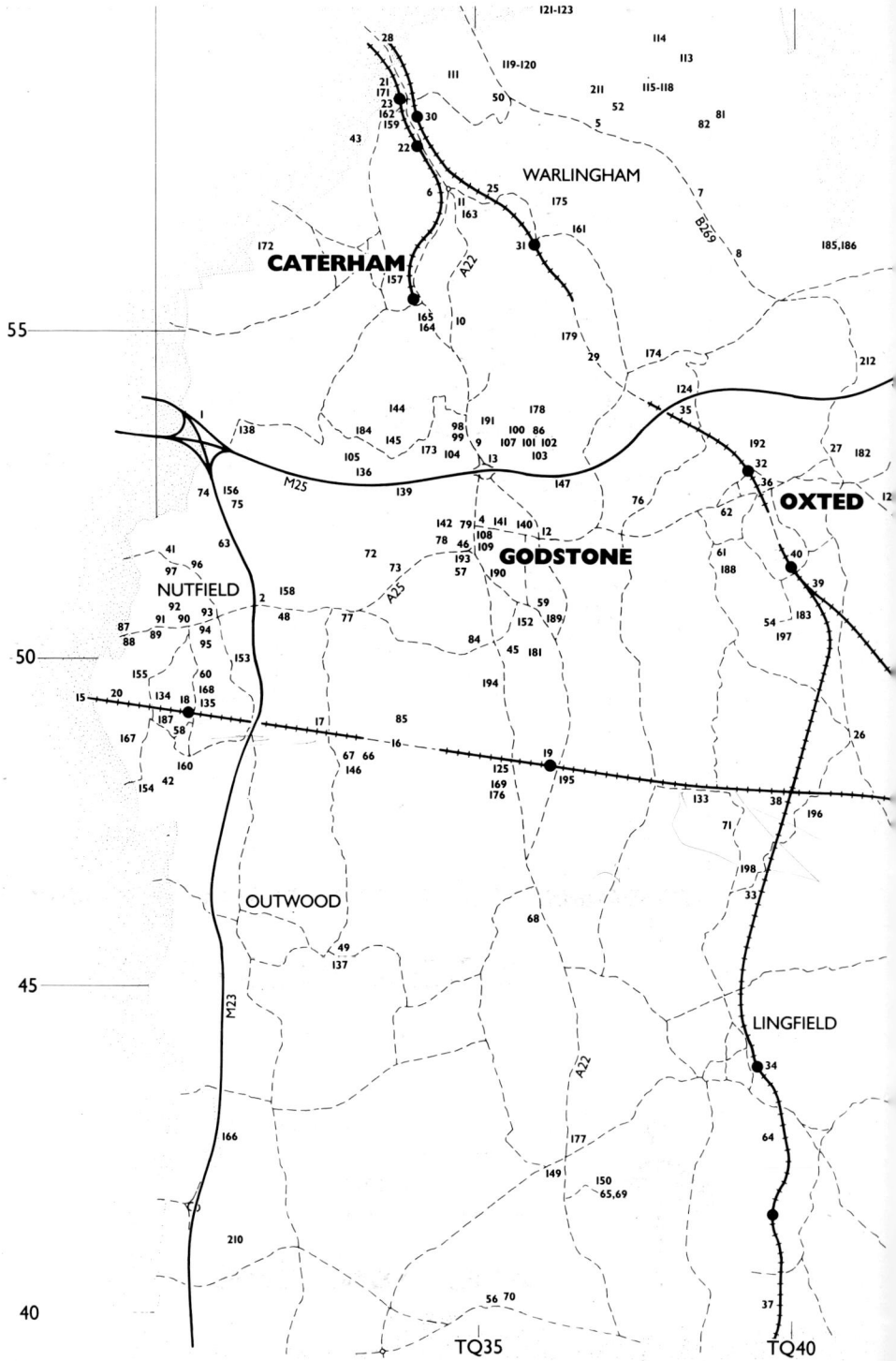

121-123

28

114

113

111

119-120

171
21
23
162
159

30

50

211

115-118

52

82

81

43

22

WARLINGHAM

6

25

11

163

175

7

B269

172

CATERHAM

31

161

8

185,186

157

A22

179

29

174

212

165
164

10

124

35

1

144

138

178

191

100   86

192

27   182

32

184

145

98
99

9

107 101 102

103

36

OXTED

105

173

104

13

147

76

62

12

136

139

74   156
75

M25

142   79

4   141   140

108

12

61

40

41

97   96

63

72

78   46   109

193   190

57

188

39

92

NUTFIELD

158

2

73

A25

59

54   183

91   90   93

48

77

152   189

197

87   88

89   94

95

GODSTONE

84

45   181

155

60

153

194

15   20

134   18   135

168

85

19

26

187

58

17

16

67   66

146

125

169
176

195

133

38

196

167

160

71

154   42

198

33

OUTWOOD

M23

49

137

68

45

LINGFIELD

A22

34

177

64

166

149

150

65,69

210

56   70

37

40

TQ35

TQ40

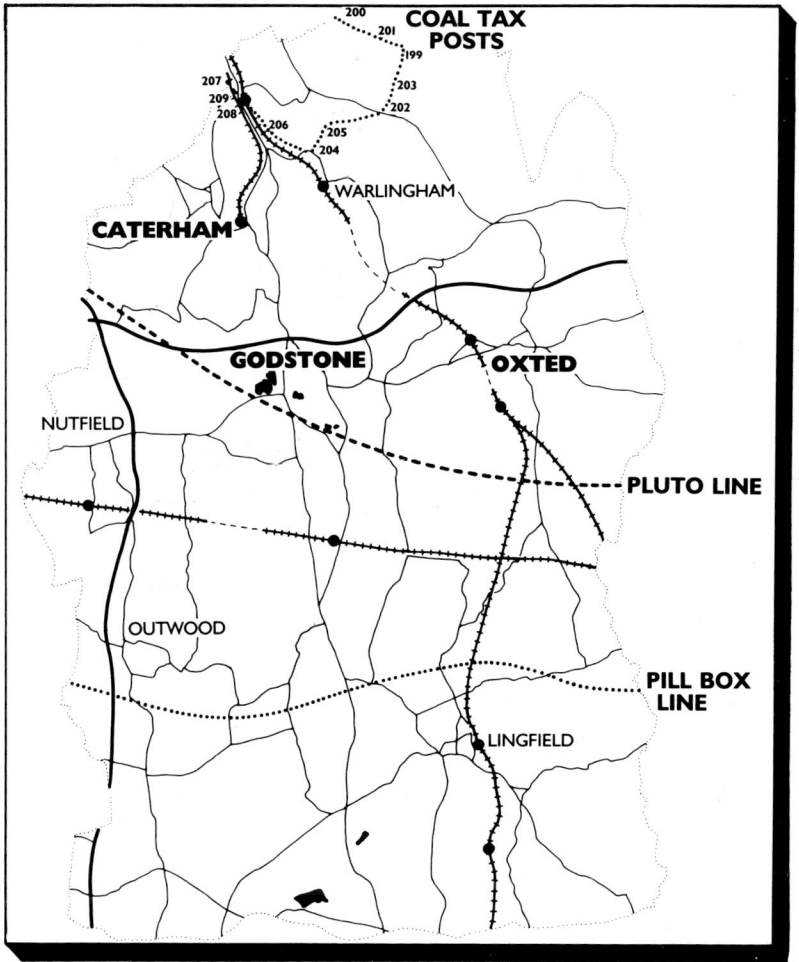

TANDRIDGE
DISTRICT

COAL TAX POSTS

200
201
199
207
209
208
203
206
202
205
204

WARLINGHAM

CATERHAM

GODSTONE

OXTED

NUTFIELD

PLUTO LINE

OUTWOOD

PILL BOX LINE

LINGFIELD

28
29

143

47   83
131-132

028

N

	TANDRIDGE BOUNDARY
	ROADS
	MOTORWAYS
	RAILWAYS

0   1   2   3   4   5km

92 SETTLING PIT

TQ 303 512 ■

North west of the site of the former Park Works is a wide shallow pit. Here the fuller's earth was allowed to settle after being ground in water. Probably this was a method of washing and grading before kiln drying. Later in the nineteenth century the dried earth was separated into different grades using air currents created by a fan.

93 NUTFIELD VILLAGE

TQ 308 501 ✳

Nutfield is a small linear village along the A25 with a few buildings dating before the nineteenth century and is intimately connected with the fuller's earth industry. Buildings composed of stone (quoinstone) from the fuller's earth pits are very evident.

North of the village and east of the football pitch is heavily worked ground.

94 WELL HOUSE

TQ 309 506 ■

Well House on the north side of High Street, Nutfield is where James Cawley (1822-1882) and his son Claude William Cawley lived. In those days it was called the Tower because a tower (which is actually a folly which still stands today) was erected in the garden.

Claude William Cawley rose to become a dominating figure in the whole of the English fuller's earth business and he was the first managing director of the Fuller's Earth Union Ltd. He also worked a hearthstone mine at Betchworth.

95 CAPENOR

TQ 313 507 ■

The area to the east of Robert Denholm House at the east end of the village of Nutfield, on the south side of the A25 was worked from 1992-1993 . In actual fact this pit was a re-working of a much earlier one and mining was recorded in 1895. Also in 1962 an experimental mine was opened. but the three 300ft headings proved to be unstable and were abandoned in 1964.

Almost the whole of the south side of the ridge between Capenor and Chartfield has been worked for the earth at one time. Most of the former pits have been used as small landfill sites but it is still possible to find traces of workings north of Priory Farm.

96 GLEBE QUARRY

TQ 307 514 ■

Work on the M23 in 1972 (not surprisingly) exposed fuller's earth when the motorway alignment intersected the A25. This stimulated extraction in the area north of the ridge between Nutfield Church and the line of the motorway. This lasted until the late 1980s.

Subsequent landscaping has left a lake at the north west corner of the site. Apart from the water, this is part of a large fuller's earth pit left in its working state.

97 PRESERVED PITS
AT *THE INN ON THE POND*

TQ 302 514 ■

Old steep sided fuller's earth pits still remain to the SW of the pub. Even up to recent times steep sided pits were a familiar feature of the landscape but most of the older ones are now filled and modern working methods do not leave such pits.

below: **Fuller's earth workers, early in the 20th century** *Photo held by Nutfield Local History Group*

In common parlance underground workings are called mines and open pits are called quarries. Strictly speaking a mine is a working where minerals are extracted, regardless of whether or not the mineral is taken from underground galleries or pits open to the sky. Likewise the term quarry should, in a strict sense, be reserved for sites where stone blocks for building purposes are cut from a suitable stratum, regardless of whether the workings are underground or in an open pit. Generally in this work the purist terminology is followed except in certain place names. It would be confusing, for example, to rename what is generally known as Arch mine to Arch quarry.

GODSTONE AREA

The Upper Greensand strata are of the order of 9m thick at Godstone and dip about 4 degrees northwards under the North Downs. Something like the top third are loose green sands and underneath there is a layer of hard 'roofstone' perhaps 40cm thick. In past times, this hard layer allowed underground digging to take place in the 1.5m of softer rock beneath. When the disused galleries are entered the rock walls appear to contain just one kind of stone. Nevertheless the stone was worked for three different purposes and each required a particular substratum of the rock face to be extracted. Generally better building blocks could be made from the stone nearer the bottom.

As far as is known the mines opened in the seventeenth century and it is assumed that building stone was a prized product. Nevertheless on account of its refractory properties the stone has long been known as 'firestone'. After the great fire of London this sort of stone, generically termed Reigate stone, was in demand for hearths. Perhaps this gave some impetus to the underground quarrying. Reports from the end of the of the nineteenth century (actually the declining years of the quarries) stress the importance of the stone in lining furnaces concerned with glass making and pottery. For this purpose the stone was removed in slabs rather than square blocks.

By the twentieth century the product from the underground workings was chiefly 'hearthstone'. At some time during the industrial revolution housewives took to the practice of smartening stone door-steps, window ledges and fireside hearths by rubbing them with lumps or blocks of 'hearthstone'. A white surface with a hint of green was produced. The east Surrey mines were a valuable source of this hearthstone and in Godstone it was the upper part of the underground working faces which yielded it.

The sale of hearthstone continued to the 1960s and it was either sold as lumps straight from the mine, or dust in sprinkler cartons. Also crushed stone from the mine was compacted with a little cement into shaped blocks. To a certain extent the hearthstone industry was a profitable way of using up waste from the extraction of stone blocks and slabs although it is undoubtedly true that older workings were extended, and new mines developed for hearthstone itself.

Hearthstone (for whitening hearths and other elements of domestic architecture made of harder stones) should not be confused with hearth-stones which as mentioned above were refractory slabs used for making domestic and industrial hearths.

The underground spaces produced by the extraction of building stone and hearthstone have been utilised for mushroom growing and storage. Usage as air-raid shelters, nuclear bomb shelters and wine storage have been proposed but not, as far as is known, implemented.

These underground workings have an important archaeological significance since they preserve relics of the local past which would not have survived on the surface. Important research has been performed by members of the Wealden Cave and Mine Society and other bodies.

For years after WWII Godstone Hill mine and Arch mine (as all local underground workings) lay derelict and became a playground for local youths. Recorded activities include riding motor bikes through Godstone Hill, holding parties in Arch Mine, and making love.

By 1993 the mines and underground quarries were carefully protected by the Wealden Cave and Mine Society as bat hibernacula. With an alarming decrease in the bat population, it has become increasingly necessary to protect the places where they hibernate and mate.

CHALDON AREA

On the western edge of Tandridge District, stretching from the intersection of the motorways to the area of Quarry Cottages and north of Rockshaw Road and Springbottom Lane, lies a complex series of ancient stone quarries dug into the 'Reigate Stone'. Some parts of these may be nearly 1000 years old and the stone had a distinguished use in medieval London. It is a very light easily carvable freestone. However it is not very durable, finds no use in the modern world and is certainly susceptible to damage by acid rain.

It is not known when underground extraction ceased in this area, although there are 17th and early 18th century inscriptions underground and also late 18th century and very early 19th century quarry leases. It is reasonable to assume that the quarrymen were prevented from extending the galleries further north, down the dip of the rock under the chalk of the North Downs, by reason of the water table obtaining in these early times. Stone extraction therefore shifted towards the Godstone area during the 17th century and in the nineteenth century pits were also dug nearer Merstham, a little to the east . Here methods were developed to drain the new quarries. The new quarries were in addition to medieval quarries also dug at Merstham.

98 GODSTONE HILL MINE

TQ 349 536

Godstone Hill mine, properly quarry, is known as 'The Main Series' by local cavers. It was formerly accessed at ground level within the chalk pit in this area. It is now accessed from a man-hole and a shallow shaft on the west side of the A22. As the A22 has developed it has been raised up and the old chalk pit floor has been buried.

Like all the underground quarries and mines in the area it was worked by the pillar and stall method. This system left substantial pillars of unworked stone at frequent intervals to support the roof.

A very large area of ground was worked and a complex system of galleries has resulted. A huge maze has resulted from the working practice which left large amounts of discarded stone and the trimmings from dressing the blocks and slabs, stacked between the pillars behind neat dry stone walls.

The system is very unstable and there have been roof-falls and pillars have cracked. Several craters or crown holes on the surface indicate collapsed workings below ground. The basic direction of digging was northwards under the downs following the dip of the rock but this was limited by the water table. The northernmost parts of the workings were always subjected to flooding and in the second part of the 20th century these flooded workings were lost behind a series of roof falls.

The appearance of the mine by 1993 had largely been fashioned by the mushroom growers who used the quarries for most of the first part of the 20th century and probably earlier. They cleared roof falls, lime-washed many of the walls and inserted pit-props (railway sleepers) in certain places.

It is possible to work out the mining methods and of particular interest are the railway systems. The earliest system is a plate way using, at least in part, plates from the Croydon Merstham and Godstone extension of the Surrey Iron Railway. These plates were used even into this century using horse-drawn (three-in-a-line) low trolleys to remove the stone. The plates were simply attached to the ground (stone block sleepers being unnecessary.) Interestingly, at the innermost ends of the plateways, it seems that the plates themselves were deemed unnecessary and the trolleys or trams were merely run along ruts in the ground.

Further evidence of the horse-drawn trams comes from grooves scored in the walls where the whipple-trees of the horse trains rubbed. The whipple-tree is the wooden cross piece which holds the traces harnessing the horses to the tram. It swings about.

Godstone Hill is the largest of the known stone mines extant in the Godstone area. It had more that one entrance. The best known was on the east side of the Roman Road at TQ 351 534 but this is now sealed against vandals. It is highly probable that it once connected underground with the adjacent Arch and Carthorse quarries.

99 ARCH MINE

TQ 348 535

The entrance to this underground quarry was originally through a brick arch at the bottom of a chalk pit which once existed in this locality and constituted the quarry yard.

In the 1950s the pit was filled with pulverised

fuel ash but access to the arch was retained by installing a deep shaft equipped with climbing rungs. Later the shaft was filled with rubble and when it was unearthed by Croydon Caving Club all the rungs were found to be destroyed. Today only properly equipped caving clubs have access. The entrance is to be found on the hillside to the west of the A22.

The interior of Arch quarry resembles Godstone Hill but there are larger expanses of unsupported roof and the activities of the mushroom growers are much more evident.

French or Belgian names, dating to 1903, have been found inscribed on the walls.

100 CARTHORSE MINE
TQ 352 536

The entrance to Carthorse is through a small square steel door set in a cliff face near the present warehouses. It is zealously protected by the its owner and access is restricted.

Carthorse was used to store wine, articles from the Natural History Museum and possibly material from London Hospitals during WWII.

Today the quarry remains in the rather neat condition it was rendered during the war and there are few signs of recent roof-falls. There is abundant evidence pertaining to its war-time uses and also suggestions that mushroom growing occurred. A narrow bricked-up air-shaft may relate to this activity.

101 MARDEN MINE
TQ 357 535

Marden mine is one of the series of underground workings high on the Downs beneath the lodge to Marden Park.

It is possibly the 'Marden New Stone Quarry' described in a lease of 1849. It was originally an underground stone quarry but this century, until 1955, it was dug as a hearthstone mine. Below ground the contrast between the galleries used for these purposes can be seen.

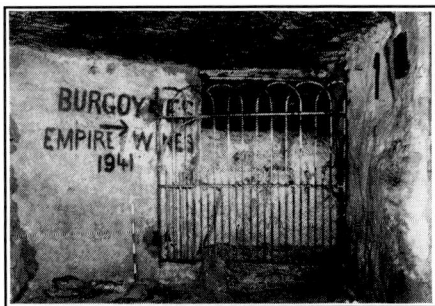

100: In Carthorse Mine, Godstone

Externally its principal features are the deep rectangular brick-lined shaft whose top is concealed near the lodge at the entrance to Marden Park; the 4 ft diameter concrete pipe which was inserted into an original mine entrance at the foot of the cliff in 1983, and a partially filled now dry well near this entrance. The concrete pipe was laid by the land owner for unknown purposes.

During WWII the older parts of this extensive quarry were used as a bonded liquor store and a Customs and Excise post was established at one of the entrances.

After the war the mine remained sealed until cavers entered it by clearing and descending the shaft in 1978. Quarrying tools were found and are preserved in the Croydon Natural History and Scientific Society Ltd's museum.

Today in Marden one can find clear spaces, brick partitions and steel doors (which are evidence of the bonded liquor store days); evidence of an early plate railway; and traces of mushroom growing which took place before WWII. More sinister are small recent roof-falls which indicate the instability of the mine.

102 COB HILL MINE
TQ 360 532

Slightly to the east of Marden quarry but still in the dell below Marden Park Lodge are the remains of a drift entrance which is assumed to lead into Cob Hill mine. This is mentioned in government mining records of 1899 but has not been entered in recent times.

103 THE GNOMEYS
TQ 3575 5353

In the vicinity of Marden and Cob Hill mines is a shallow series of short disconnected subterranean passages in very soft rock which have been dubbed 'The Gnomeys'. Their purpose is not known.

104 BALDWYN'S FOLLY
TQ 348 532

Baldwyn's Folly offers a salutary warning about the instability of the hearthstone mines. Started during the last century the entrance was deliberately collapsed in 1931 by the council as it posed a hazard to adventurous boys. Before this a collapse had caused a large crater in the field above which was locally dubbed the cup. It was described as being heavily timbered inside. The remains of a drift entrance beside the sunken track at **TQ 348 532** are the only trace of it.

105 QUARRY HANGERS
TQ 322 536

The house, Quarry Hangers, is sited at an abandoned chalk pit. It is known that there are stone mines below it but efforts by local caving clubs over the years to find a way in have failed.

106 CHALDON BOTTOM
TQ 308 537

There are about 17 kilometres of galleries constituting this underground system which is associated with medieval and later times up to the eighteenth century. The most surprising feature is the stability of the system and most of it has survived to this day, although some was lost during the construction of the M23 motorway.

It was sealed up and virtually lost and forgotten until caving clubs rediscovered it in 1967. From that time it has been the subject of much historical and archaeological research and in view of its importance, it is now under consideration for scheduling as a statutory scheduled ancient monument.

With the assistance of The Wealden Cave and Mine Society it is sometimes possible to visit it, and apart from the experience of caving which this entails, stone quarrying techniques stretching from medieval times to the eighteenth century may be studied.

Unlike the Godstone area, the underground galleries were not dug into a hillside but into a small artificial face produced by sinking a pit into the ground. There are several associated with the system but the best example is at Bedlam's Bank.

107 WINDERS HILL MINE
TQ 354 535

An entrance to this underground system can be clearly seen under the track way which leads from Godstone to Marden Park. It was once the eastern end of a short tramway which led downhill. Attempts to dig into it by local cavers have largely been defeated by old roof-falls. Nevertheless a small area underground is accessible but it is on private property.

II MINES IN THE LOWER GREENSAND

Godstone is largely built on the Folkestone beds of the Lower Greensand. Digging for sand has occurred within the village from last century until recent times. Unlike the upper part of the sand which is stained with iron, the lower part is white and is known as silver sand. This is a very fine grained sand which flows freely when dry. During the 19th century and in the early years of the 20th century the silver sand was extracted underground by the pillar and stall method.

Former uses of silver sand include, as a cleaning (scouring) powder, for lining floors before the days of affordable floor coverings, as a 'blotting paper', for hour-glasses, and for glass making.

108 FAIRALLS, GODSTONE
TQ 350 519

Subterranean workings occurred in the vicinity of the present day Fairalls Ltd. (a long established builders merchants) which is near the high point on the west side of Godstone High Street. It is unlikely that any caverns now exist either because they were worked away when the upper parts of the sand was removed, or they have been lost through collapse. The cavity revealed when Fairalls needed to extend their warehouse in 1988 was filled.

109 No 45-47 HIGH STREET, GODSTONE
TQ 350 519

There was once an illicit trade in the silver sand, and small workings can be found underneath the buildings of the High Street. A mines system stretching eastward is still to be found behind 45-47 High Street Godstone.

The scarp face of the North Downs is scarred with the remains of numerous chalk pits about which there is little documentary information despite the fact that they were dug in quite recent times.

There were extensive workings at Godstone Hill, which were filled with pulverised fuel ash, PFA, from Croydon power station in about 1955, and the large pits at Oxted linger on at a low level of operational use.

The purpose of these pits was to extract chalk for 'burning' to lime. Increasing quantities of lime were needed for building projects in the nineteenth century and large amounts were needed for agricultural purposes. Industrial uses such as gas purification, water softening, tanning and sugar refining were also important.

Chalk, which is calcium carbonate, decomposes to quicklime, which is calcium oxide, when burnt. This is a reactive substance which reacts violently with water to produce hydrated lime or slaked lime, chemically known as calcium hydroxide. Hydrated lime has two valuable properties. Firstly it is a finely divided alkaline powder, which means it can be spread evenly on the land for agricultural purposes. By counteracting the acidity, making the soil porous and providing calcium, it improves the fertility of clay soils. A finely divided powder is most effective for this purpose.

The second valuable property of hydrated lime is that, it slowly reverts to calcium carbonate under the influence of water and carbon dioxide which is always present in the atmosphere and the soil. In the building trade lime was originally delivered as quicklime and slaked with water to produce lime putty. For the bricklayers this was mixed with sand to produce mortar. The mortar strengthened with time as the calcium hydroxide slowly reverted to calcium carbonate.

From about the 1920s limeworks increasingly developed hydrating plants and sold 'hydrated' rather than 'quick' lime. This released the end user from the unpleasant job of 'slaking'.

A better hydrated lime, semi-hydraulic lime, was produced when the impure lower chalk from the pits was burned. This was because it was contaminated with clay which provided hard stable insoluble silicates and alumina as the mortar set. Thus a stronger mortar was produced.

124: Oxted lime kilns in the first half of the 20th century   *Photo held by Malcolm Tadd*

110-123 DENE HOLES

Before modern times, farmers on the clay soils on the dip slopes of the downs would sink narrow shafts through the superincumbent 'clay with flints', Thanet sand, or other geologically younger deposits, and mine the chalk from small chambers at the bottom. These small chalk mines are known as dene holes. The tradition dates back for hundreds, perhaps thousands of years. Pliny the elder describes them in 70 AD. In the 17th century the style of workmanship in constructing the holes became less elaborate and these later dene holes are known as chalk wells. Chalk wells are wider and shallower.

The chalk itself was used as a soil improver but in later days it was often burnt to lime, in small kilns, constructed to serve the needs of an individual farmer.

Dene holes are well known, and often easily identifiable in Kent and Essex, but their existence can only be inferred in Surrey. The method is to find craters and depressions in locations which resemble areas of Kent and Essex which are rich in deneholes. These are near old field boundaries and near the edges of present or former woods.

Possible denehole sites have been located at Crewes Avenue (**Site 110**, TQ 355 592) and Tithe Pit Shaw Lane (**Site 111**, TQ 346 589), Warlingham. Also Hagglers Dean, Farleigh, (**Site 112**, TQ 371 614) and in the Chelsham area–**Sites 113-123**: TQ 381593, TQ 376 594, TQ 372 585, TQ 372 584, TQ 372 584, TQ 374 584, TQ 356 593, TQ 356 593, TQ 357 598, TQ 358 599, TQ 361 597.

124 OXTED CHALK PIT

TQ 383 544 ■

Opened in the 19th century the chalk pit at Oxted is extensive. A company was incorporated to run it in 1885 and in 1932 it was being run by the Oxted Greystone Lime Co. Limited and that year commercial liaison started with the Dorking Greystone Lime Co. Limited.

At present (1993) it is owned by Tilcon but their operations are confined to the west side of Chalk Pit Lane. The floor of the pit is actively dug on a daily basis for the chalk although the pit, which could be claimed to be the most prominent and familiar landmark in east Surrey, is greening over in parts.

For a period up to the beginning of 1993 Tilcon's chief activity on the site was to hydrate burnt lime (quick lime or calcium oxide), which

is brought in bulk by road from another of the company's sites near Skipton in Yorkshire. The hydrating plant was cleverly designed to be operated by one man as a continuous process. In a tall building, water was introduced to a moving stream of burnt lime. The consequent stream of hydrated lime was carried aloft and then passed to Sturtevant separators which took out the finely divided hydrated lime (slaked lime or calcium hydroxide) and conveyed it to bunkers to await removal from the site in bulk container vehicles. The coarser hydrated lime, which was rejected by the separator was pulverised and passed to a second separator. This increased the yield of the finer hydrated lime and the small amount rejected was discarded to the ground outside the plant.

The hydrated lime was for use chiefly by Tilcon itself which is a company heavily involved in the construction industry. Hydrated lime improves sand and cement mortars and is used in plasters.

In 1993 the Oxted pit was still serving agricultural needs. Chalk was being dug and crushed and screened and dried for high quality agricultural 'lime' and was one of only a few operations in Kent and Surrey which could produce the high quality ground lime for essential soil fertilisation.

The chalk, as dug, was also being used as a path and road base material and as a general fill product.

Nine lime kilns remain from the pit's lime burning days of about 20 years ago. There are the remains of a battery of six 'Oxted Kilns'. Because the tops of two of these are broken down only four can be seen on the skyline. The remaining four appear as brick cylinders strengthened with iron hoops. They were fed from the top. Originally chalk was brought from the chalk face in skips (three at a time) on rails, to the platform at the top of the kilns. (One of the skips remains on the site.) Eventually lorries replaced the skips and a chalk crushing plant was installed near the tops of the kilns. This is still there. The kilns were fed, at their tops, by a digger, Ruston No.4. running on rails. Traces of the rails remain.

In operation only five of the six kilns were fired at one time. The sixth would be under repair and maintenance. Adjacent to the battery of kilns, now half buried, is the derelict former

124: Oxted lime kilns early in the 20th century

Drawing by Peter Watkins based on photograph in Roger Packham Collection

bricklayers' hut. The brickwork of the kilns required constant maintenance.

The kilns were fired with one part of coke to five parts of chalk fed from the top. The chalk had to be carefully graded. If the lumps were too small they would choke the kiln. Lime works are always associated with mounds of discarded chalk.

An unusual kiln at the west end of the battery of six is a steel kiln. It is about the same size as the brick kilns and was fired by oil. Chalk was poured through a steel door at the top and lime was taken out at the bottom. It does not seem to have been successful.

The remaining two kilns are 'Brockham' kilns. The site was once served by a railway siding from the Oxted line. There is little trace of this now but it is possible to discern the point where it connected with the Oxted line on the south side of the M25.

As is usual with such pits, in 1993 the Oxted pit is registered as a land-fill site but it is used only for the company's relatively small needs.

13   BRICK MAKING AND POTTERIES

Bricks are made by moulding clay into shape, drying and firing in a kiln at 950-1150 deg. centigrade.

If coke breeze, anthracite dust or town ash containing unburnt coal is added to the clay, the bricks themselves ignite which assists the kilning process.

Stock bricks are moulded by pushing soft clay (soft mud) into multiple moulds. In the wirecut process a column of stiff clay is extruded and cut into bricks by pushing through a wire frame.

In Tandridge District opportunity for brick making is afforded by the Gault clay, Clay with Flints, and Weald clay. Of these there is no evidence that the Gault has been utilised.

On Limpsfield Common, clays (brick earth) associated with the Sandgate Beds have also been worked to produce bricks.

Bricks were often produced in clamps in which they were fired in stacks enclosed with old bricks and turfs. The presence of ponds adjacent to old houses in the Weald can indicate the place where the clay was extracted to produce the bricks, which were made in a clamp, to build the house. It is also possible to find gaps between houses in Victorian housing developments where the clamps once stood.

Pottery making occurred in Tandridge but information about it is very scanty.

125 LAMB'S BRICKWORKS, SOUTH GODSTONE

TQ 349 484

This site is reached by turning off the west side of Tilburstow Hill along a minor road on the south side of the railway embankment.

The site was acquired by the Trollope family in about 1895. It had previously been a pottery. A wirecut brickworks was built which consisted of a boiler, a steam engine, a continuous kiln with a square chimney, three beehive kilns and a rectangular kiln. The bricks were dried before kilning with exhausted steam from the engine.

During WWI the site was requisitioned for use as a large ammunition dump by the military.

The Lamb family acquired the site in 1919 when new plant for stiff plastic bricks was installed. This included 2 German submarine engines to generate electricity.

In 1920 production of hand made roofing tiles was started.

A new kiln with a round chimney slightly higher than the square one was built.

The manufacturing capacity was further in-creased in 1936 by the installation of Berry machines to produce stock bricks.

During WWII the plant was once again requisitioned–this time for the Canadian Army who used it as a Royal Armament Depot for the repair of tanks and general armaments.

Production of handmade tiles was not con-tinued after the war because of competition from concrete tiles. The manufacture of stiff plastic bricks ceased in 1964, also because of severe competition.

The business was thriving in 1993 but for stock bricks only. The following describes the process.

Water, Weald clay, spent fuel from fluidised bed furnaces (purchased from, among other firms, Reeds paper mills and Tate and Lyles') is blended. The plastic mixture is conveyed by belts to a machine which presses it into brick shaped wooden moulds after coating the moulds with sand. The soft bricks are then dropped out of the moulds onto trolleys and pushed along rail tracks to special drying sheds, where they are dried for days before delivery to the kilns. The dried bricks are stacked in the

125: Lambs brickworks, South Godstone

Photo: Chris Shepheard

kilns (clamps) which are then sealed at their fronts with waste bricks and sand. The kilns are fired with gas jets set in their backs. At the high temperature produced (1100 deg. C.) the small amounts of residual fuel (coal) incorporated into the bricks ignite and play their part in producing the black and red mottled bricks.

In 1993 it is pleasing to note that an up-to-date plant stands in a modern business park built from redundant parts of the site and its buildings. A fine example of a long-standing local business adapting to modern times.

The works owes its existence to its clay pits in the deep stratum of Wealden clay. A test bore in 1926 proved the seam to be 365 feet thick.

The railway siding which once served the works is still in existence but is now used by British Railways for the disposal and part recovery of railway ballast in redundant clay pits. It was closed in the early 1960s but later reopened.

126–127 LIMPSFIELD BRICK WORKS
TQ 412 523 ■

There was a brick works on Limpsfield Common until the beginning of the 20th century which could be part of a local tradition dating back to the 18th century. Red bricks and tiles were manufactured, although it is said that grey stock bricks were also produced. The bricks may be seen locally incorporated into door and window frames but the locally dug stone was cheaper than bricks and the older local houses are largely built of this stone.

A pit where the brick-earth was dug is to be found on the golf course in Brick Kiln Lane. The brick-earth was mixed with Weald Clay, brought from a distance to make the bricks.

Site 127, (TQ 412 524), Links Cottage was the manager's house.

128–132 POTTERIES IN THE LIMPSFIELD AREA ■

There was a medieval pottery industry in the Limpsfield area which was believed to have flourished in the years 1250-1350. It served the Reigate and Croydon areas and the pottery was hand-made without the use of a wheel.

Excavations for the construction of the M25 motorway service station at Clacket Lane, (**site 128**, TQ 423 545) 1991-1993, revealed two different pottery sites. Kiln sites had previously been identified at Westwood Farm (**site 129**, TQ 428 539), in the vicinity of Watts Hill (**site 130**, TQ 424 528), in the vicinity of

Scearn Bank (**site 131**, TQ 429 515) and at Ridlands Farm.

The dark grey banks of waste at Scearn Bank, (**site 132**, TQ 430 516), were created by this industry.

33 REDLAND BRICK LIMITED, CROWHURST
TQ 394 464 ■

Brick making (wirecut) ceased on this site, which is on the Wealden clay, in 1979 but bricks were still stored. The line of the former railway siding to the Oxted line (which was closed in the 1950s when the works changed fuel from coal to oil) was visible in 1993.

The Staffordshire continuous kiln with chambers (variously quoted as 14, 16 or 22 in number) was still standing in 1993. The Staffordshire kiln resembles a Hoffmann kiln in which the kilns are set round an endless circle. While one kiln is firing two or three ahead of it are being prepared. This means that when the first is closed the next in line can be fired immediately. The tall central chimney which served all the kilns had gone by 1993. Only the boiler house chimney remained. A deep flooded pit still remained in 1993 but another (more recent) was being used as a landfill site.

133 BRICK AND TILE WORKS, CROWHURST LANE EAST
TQ 381 480

Nothing remains of these works which were at Brickmakers' Wood. Clay was dug from a pit at **TQ 3855 4775** (now filled) and shipped by tramway down to the works. It was still possible in 1993 to discern where the tramway passed through the woods.

134 BRICK AND TILE WORKS, SOUTH NUTFIELD
TQ 301 490

This site operated until about the beginning of the 20th century but eventually became used by the Nutfield Manufacturing Co. Ltd.

See Chapter 21, page 47

135 MEDIEVAL POTTERY KILN, SOUTH NUTFIELD
TQ 310 492 ■

A medieval kiln was detected on this site (north of railway line on east side of village) in the 1960s.

The plateau on the dip slope of the North Downs has a history of water scarcity. For example before 1857 the water supply for Chaldon was at the bottom of White Hill and had to be carried up the steep scarp slope of the North Downs using yokes and pails. Some sort of water cistern could still be found in 1993, north of the A25 on the bank at the west side of White Hill, (**site 136, TQ 326 530**).

Elsewhere in Tandridge District water is plentiful, as large numbers of wells, road side springs and ponds demonstrate. Despite this there is a modern covered reservoir (**site 137**, TQ 327 452) at Outwood which is used by the East Surrey Water Company to store water imported from Kent and other reservoirs on the North Downs and the Greensand ridge.

The Vale of Holmsdale, between the North Downs and the Greensand ridge is a very important water resource. Wells are sunk into the Lower Greensand strata in which it accumulates since the underlying Weald Clay forms a water impermeable barrier. The dreary looking brick buildings surrounded by security fences which are to be found along the route of the M25 house the East Surrey Water Company's pumps. At Godstone the Company's water treatment plant is to be found.

138-140 EAST SURREY WATER COMPANY PUMP HOUSES

Site 138, TQ 313 537 ■
Site 139, TQ 319 528 ■
Site 140, TQ 358 524 ■
See also **site 212**, TQ 410 542

141 TREATMENT WORKS
TQ 353 522 ■

The treatment works is near the junction of the Oxted Road and the road (A22) through Godstone. Its water aeration fountains were still making an interesting, almost pretty, sight in 1993.

142 OPEN SAND PIT
TQ 346 519 ■

This pit NW of the *Hare and Hounds* at Godstone, and the adjacent pit to the east, were adopted as East Surrey Water Company open reservoirs but in 1993 were being filled with inert materials. The water company considered them to be too easily polluted. This is a pity for not only had they become attractive nature reserves but they served to demonstrate the depth of the water table in a steep sided pit.

143 144 137 RESERVOIRS

Underground reservoirs are at Outwood **TQ 327 452** (**site 137**) where water from the River Eden is stored and on the Lower Greensand ridge almost on the border with Kent (**site 143**, TQ 436 515). A third is to be found north of *The Harrow* public house in Stanstead Road in Caterham on the Hill, (**site 144**, TQ 331 546).

145 WATER TOWER GRAVELLY HILL, CATERHAM
TQ 337 533 ■

This red brick water tower was built by East Surrey Water Company in 1897 and dominates the landscape south of the North Downs.

141: Godstone water treatment works　　　　　　　*Photo: Chris Shepheard*

146 GAS WELL

TQ 327 488

In the 1960s natural gas was struck by drilling near the west portal of the Bletchingley tunnel. For a while this was flared off rather than commercially exploited. The sealed well head was still visible in 1993, near the south side of the cutting, leading to the tunnel, where Outwood Lane crosses the railway line.

GAS PIPELINES

Gas pipelines carrying natural gas were laid across the district by SEGAS in the period 1965-1971. One system ran from Farleigh to Kenley aerodrome and another entered the district at Tatsfield, then descended the North Downs at Woldingham to finds its way to Merstham along the Upper Greensand.

147 OIL WELL

TQ 364 525

An oil well was opened at Palmer's Wood, Godstone in about 1991.

OIL PIPELINE

Esso have a network of pipelines connecting their refinery at Fawley to terminals in the north of England, the Midlands, Wales and London. Between 1981 and 1982 an extension of the pipeline which connected Fawley to the west London terminal was built. It branched off at Alton in Hampshire and terminated at Purfleet after following a devious course which took in Gatwick. Along this line it is possible to pump batches of various grades of refined oils and petroleum without them mixing.

It is quite easy to trace this pipeline across Tandridge District by means of roadside markers. The reader is left to perform this exercise on his or her own but as a clue there is one marker at Lamb's Brick Works, South Godstone.

See also **site 170**: PLUTO pipeline.

148 THE WARLINGHAM BOREHOLE

TQ 348 572

Between 1956 and 1958 one of the deepest boreholes in Tandridge District was bored for the British Geological Survey. It was 750 feet deep and 15.25 inches in diameter.

The site was in a field near Wapses Lodge roundabout on the A22 at the north end of the Caterham by-pass. (Beside the Woldingham Road, 900 yards north and 55 degrees west of Birchwood House.)

The object was to investigate a 'low gravity anomaly' in the vicinity, which might have indicated the presence of oil or coal. In the event no significant quantities of either were found, merely thick developments of Wealden and Jurassic beds.

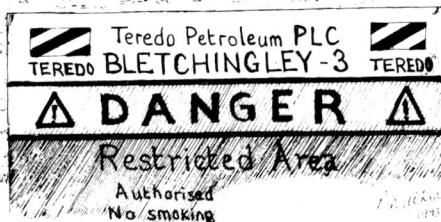

146: Gas well at Pound Hill, Bletchingley
Drawing by Peter Watkins

The Second World War had considerable impact on the district in several phases, and sites associated with these phases can be identified.

Firstly there were preparations for the war, secondly there were defences constructed in case of invasion, thirdly there was actual aerial warfare and finally there were the preparations for the allied invasion of Europe. This last phase is associated with the large number of Canadian soldiers stationed in the locality.

149 HOBBS BARRACKS. FELBRIDGE
TQ 363 415

The expansion of the army just before WWII caused Hobbs Barracks to be erected just to the south of Newchapel opposite Golards Farm. Mainly composed of wooden huts it survived in use until 1970. In 1972 it was used as a refuge for dispossessed Ugandan Asians. In 1993 it had become a highly secure private business park.

150 BAKERY, FELBRIDGE
TQ 367 419   ■

To meet the needs of the troops engaged in combat in Belgium and France at the start of WWII a large army bakery (No 1 Static Bakery) at which 10 ovens were in continuous use was established on a site adjoining the London Road, north of Wire Mill Lane. After the retreat from the continent in 1940 this bakery served a large area of south east England.

151 PILLBOXES,
MAY-SEPTEMBER 1940
TQ 299 450 to TQ 432 451

Following the defeat of the British army on the continent in 1940 hasty preparations were made for the expected invasion of southern England.

Remembering the effectiveness of the German concrete machine gun pillboxes in 1917, General Sir Edmund Ironside ordered the construction of a complex series of lines of pillboxes throughout the land. The line running through Tandridge District and which is in the rather flat area in the south of the district, was part of the General Head Quarters Line (GHQ) which stretched from the Bristol channel to the Thames estuary. The pillboxes were about 100m apart therefore constituted an uninterrupted line of defence but neverthe-less they presented rather prominent targets to the enemy. It would have helped if they had been earthed over as was the case in Belgium. Basically the line was an anti-tank defence and

in front were either water courses or an anti-tank ditch (which remains only in local memory), and barbed wire obstructions. Those required to man the line were instructed not to regard it as last ditch defence. If enemy infantry got close enough to use grenades and flame throwers the pillboxes were to be evacuated.

In construction the basic protective properties of concrete were enlisted. The brick coverings not only added to the strength of the construction but acted as shuttering during the building process. Local Royal Engineer com-manders enlisted local builders for the job.

Most of the pillboxes still stand in reasonably good condition. In general only the brickwork has deteriorated over time.

Visitors today will find two types; the infantry type and the anti-tank type which has an open front to accommodate the anti-tank guns.

In theory the pillboxes and hills of the North Downs and the Greensand ridge constituted a sound defensive system but in practice they would have been of little use because the defeated British army had lost nearly all of its arms and equipment, particularly its anti-tank guns in France and Belgium.

Some pillboxes are outside the GHQ line.

A pillbox which faces north is to be found to the north of Redhill aerodrome. Close by is a structure which resembles a pillbox from a distance but is in reality a brick wall enclosing an hexagonal area the size of a pillbox. At a third site nearby a pile of brick and concrete rubble seems to indicate the former presence of a pillbox or brick-walled enclosure.

A pillbox also stands at Anglefield corner where Tilburstow Hill meets the A22 (**site 151**, TQ 358 468).

152 ANTI-TANK OBSTACLES
AT ENTERDENT
TQ 358 508   ✱

The pyramidal concrete anti-tank blocks formerly known as dragons teeth to the public at large and as pimples to the military are rare to find in the district. However there is a line at The Enterdent which presumably filled a gap in the defences of Godstone which is otherwise protected by a series of ponds and lakes.

153 ROYAL OBSERVER CORPS POST AT BLETCHINGLEY
TQ 312 501 ■

The function of the tiny ROC posts during WWII was to watch for enemy air-craft and report to a central control so that their courses across southern England could be plotted. There was one such on Steners Hill which is an outlier from the Lower Greensand ridge south of Bletchingley and affords very extensive views to the south. No trace of this remains.

154 ROYAL OBSERVER POST AT REDHILL AERODROME
TQ 296 481

This was one of the permanent posts which was utilised for post WWII service. It was removed after the disbandment of the ROC.

155 NARROW ROAD AT SANDY LANE, NUTFIELD
TQ 305 502 ✳

The Greensand ridge between Redhill and Godstone constituted a defensive line and roads running north-south over it are generally steep and sunken between high sided banks. An exception to this rule is Sandy Lane, Nutfield. Here the road follows a shallow gradient up to Nutfield and during the war its width was deliberately restricted, by the military, by erecting a low wall on the east side. This obstruction causes inconvenience to this day.

156 OPERATIONS ROOM, BLETCHINGLEY
TQ 309 524 ■

When the M23 was constructed it severed a WWII site at Pendell Camp. This military camp was started in 1938 and was associated with a searchlight battery. For some time after the war, huts on the site were used for non-military purposes. In 1961 the inhabitants of Tristan da Cuna were evacuated there because their island was threatened by volcanic action. After the arrival of the motorway, Gipsies took over the eastern part of the site.

On the western part of the site, a military bunker still exists in an active state. This is presumably the WWII operations room but refurbished for nuclear war.

In the book, *War Plan UK*, by Duncan Campbell (1983), the site is described as originally an anti-aircraft operations room, but as the Metropolitan Police War HQ (South) in its latter day use.

157 AIR-RAID SHELTER AT CATERHAM
TQ 339 557 ■

In the bank beneath 77 Stafford Road, a small sealed-up air-raid shelter still remains. Until 1993 it was easy to find, but now the entrance is earthed up and it can now only be identified by a few courses of bricks protruding above the surface of the bank.

158 AIR-RAID SHELTER AT BLETCHINGLEY
TQ 320 512

There is a subterranean air-raid shelter in the garden of Tilgates, Bletchingley. Steps lead down to it between concrete walls.

159 AIR-RAID SHELTERS NEAR KENLEY AERODROME
TQ 333 572 ✳

To the south east of Kenley aerodrome there is a triangular grass area between, Salmons Lane, Salmons Lane West and Whyteleafe Hill. During WWII there were temporary huts used by the RAF and also a public air-raid shelter. It may be that the shallow mounds visible in this area are the site of the air-raid shelters.

160 AIR-RAID SHELTERS AT REDHILL AERODROME
TQ 300 480

Four air-raid shelters have been identified at Redhill Aerodrome. One of them is used as storage by a small factory.

161 AIR-RAID SHELTER AT WOLDINGHAM GREEN
TQ 371 556 ✳

Although sealed up under the Green this is believed to be intact.

162–164 SMALL CONCRETE WAR-TIME STRUCTURES OF UNKNOWN PURPOSE
Site 162, TQ 338 584✳, site 163, TQ 345 569✳ and site 164, TQ 346 547✳

These are small rectangular concrete structures with peep holes and wooden doors. There is one (**site 164**) at the Godstone end of the Caterham bypass on the east side of Godstone Road opposite Markville Gardens. There is another one (**site 163**) on the south side of the junction of Tillingdown Hill and Croydon Road in Caterham itself. Until 1993 there was a third (**site 164**) in Whyteleafe Hill adjacent to the still standing coal tax post.

165 RAF OPERATIONS CENTRE
TQ 342 554 ■

Kenley aerodrome was severely damaged on 18th August 1940 by a force of low flying German Dorniers and Junkers JU88 dive bombers but this had little military significance. Afterwards the vulnerable sector operations building (demolished 1980) was vacated and its function transferred on 3 September 1940 to Spice and Wallis's empty butcher's premises at 11 Godstone Road, Caterham. This building thereby became one of the most important sites in Britain at the height of the Battle on Britain. It was only used until November 1940 when a more suitable house, The Grange, Old Coulsdon replaced its function. No.11 survived the war, but not later property development, and on its site now stands a modern brick shop with a blue plaque installed by the Bourne Society which commemorates its connection with the Battle of Britain.

166 SMALLFIELD HOSPITAL
TQ 311 431 ✱

During the later years of WWII up to the invasion of Normandy in June 1944, a large area of southern England including parts of the Tandridge area were used to accommodate

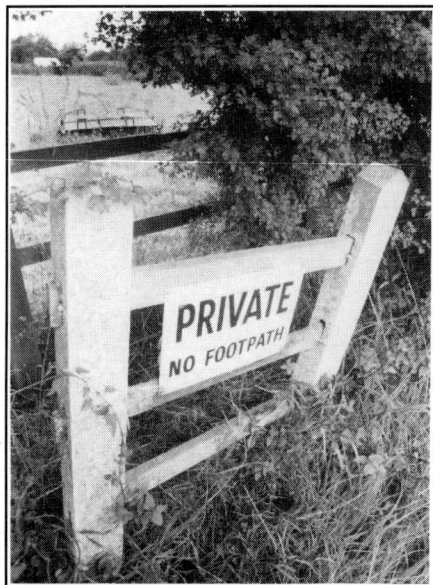

170: A marker at Godstone for the pipeline which
42 served the wartime PLUTO system

Photo: Chris Shepheard

Canadian soldiers. Buildings and engineering projects still remain from this era. Chief amongst these was Smallfield Hospital which was to be of service in treating casualties resulting from the battle for Europe 1944-1945. The casualties were flown to Redhill aerodrome and thence transported to Smallfield. The Canadian Casualty Evacuation Unit moved into Redhill Aerodrome in December 1944 for that purpose.

After the war the National Health Service took over the hospital and it gave distinguished service until the East Surrey Hospital (**TQ 284 482**) was opened at the beginning of the 1980s. Smallfield hospital stood empty until 1993 when it was demolished and a housing estate built on the site.

167 CANADIAN ROAD
TQ 298 491 to TQ 284 482 ■

The East Surrey Hospital stands at the end of a concrete road built by the Canadian forces and which never found use after the war. It runs from South Nutfield (**TQ 298 491**) and although its original purpose is obscure it would have formed a bypass around Redhill linking the A25 and A23.

168 CONCRETE BUILDINGS, SOUTH NUTFIELD
TQ 307 487

A group of concrete war-time buildings still stands hidden east of Mid Street, South Nutfield.

169 TANK DEPOT, SOUTH GODSTONE
TQ 349 484 ■

Lamb's Brickworks were requisitioned during WWII and used as a Royal Armament depot by the Canadians to repair tanks and general armaments.

170 PLUTO
TQ 312 533 to TQ 404 502 ✱

For the invasion of Europe on D-Day, 6 June 1944 it was necessary to provide the tens of thousands of vehicles landed on the beaches on Normandy in the first few days with large quantities of fuel. In preparation for this, flexible 3 inch diameter pipes were invented which could be fabricated in lengths sufficient to be laid like submarine cables across the channel in a few hours. The routes across the English Channel are from the Isle of Wight to Cherbourg and from Dungeness to Boulogne. The military code name for the system was PLUTO–Pipe Line Under the Ocean.

The fuel to the English terminals was provided by underground pipelines along which petroleum, from principally Avonmouth in the west of England, could be pumped. The route to Dungeness passes through Tandridge District and some of it is very easy to trace. It is marked with characteristic concrete posts which are generally painted white. To the untutored eye they resemble neglected fence posts. Otherwise they are immediately recognisable.

In the event PLUTO was not available for D-Day but had to await the fall of Cherbourg. It was not therefore in position until 41 days after D-Day. The lines to Boulogne were not in operation until almost 1945 and played no part at all in the actual invasion.

In 1993 the pipe-lines for PLUTO was still in use but an ESSO underground pipe line had also been laid across Tandridge.

171 ST. LUKE'S CHURCH, WHYTELEAFE
TQ 337 583   *

This contains war graves with memorial stones of the type designed for the War Graves Commission on the western front. The graves are of airmen from Kenley and a significant proportion died in the Battle of Britain year 1940. There are other types of head stones mainly to airmen who died before WWII as the result of accidents.

17   MILITARY SITES OTHER THAN OF THE SECOND WORLD WAR

Military events before the Second World War made little impact on Tandridge District.

172 CATERHAM BARRACKS
TQ 322 565   ■

This was built in 1875-7 to train soldiers from the regiments which constituted the Brigade of Guards. It was known as the Guards Depot but its function was transferred to Pirbright in 1966 and abolished as such in 1993.

173 PILGRIM'S FORT, FOSTER DOWN, CATERHAM
TQ 344 533   ■

In the late 1880s the military authorities began to have doubts about the protection of England against invasion being left solely in the hands of the Royal Navy.

The French were considered to be the potential aggressor and a plan was drawn up to construct a system of entrenchments around London should the Royal Navy fail to prevent a landing. The plan consisted of constructing a series of mobilisation centres which were to store ammunition and trench digging tools. The trenches were only to be dug if hostilities broke out.

The 13 mobilisation centres were built between 1893 and 1902 but when they finally emerged they looked very like forts. This was not what the public and Parliament were expecting! The circular one at Foster Down was in fact an infantry redoubt with a rifle parapet on a rampart covering a **V** ditch with a fence at its bottom. It commanded the high ground and its magazines were underground. Outside there was a barn-like structure for storage and a caretaker's cottage.

The scheme was abolished in about 1906 but apart from the fort at Denbies near Dorking all the structures are still in existence.

174 WOLDINGHAM ARTILLERY MAGAZINES
TQ 379 546

As part of the 1880s scheme two unfortified artillery magazines were built on The Ridge north of Oxted Lime Works. They are both still there but one has a house built on it. They lie back from The Ridge a few metres to the east of Southview road. There is a group of houses, and the magazines lie in the grounds of Flemings which is private. Other houses in the vicinity are named, Fort Garth, Fort Lodge and Fort Cottage. On The Ridge itself are concrete posts inscribed, **WD4** and **WD5**.   **43**

175 WOLDINGHAM GARDEN VILLAGE

TQ 363 570   ✱

The army built a camp on the site of what is now Woldingham Garden Village (Muscombes field) in 1914. It became the quarters for the Public Schools Battalion of the Middlesex Regiment. However in 1916 it was adopted as a wounded soldiers' convalescent home but it finally closed in April 1919 and was sold to Henry F Morris for development as a Garden Village in 1920.

In 1993 it is a mixture of original WWI army huts adapted for modern residential living and later houses. At least one converted bungalow (19 Hill Top) still retains its original timber walls, and in the garden is a shed built of corrugated iron said to be from the original camp wash-house.

Woldingham Garden Village is a quaint corner of the district and since there is only one road leading into it, and it is not on a through route, its in habitants enjoy an undisturbed existence.

176 AMMUNITION STORE, LAMB'S BRICK WORKS, SOUTH GODSTONE

TQ 349 484

Lamb's brickworks was requisitioned as a an ammunition and explosives store during World War I. At that time it belonged to the Trollope family but was sold to the Lamb family in 1919.

177 LANDING STRIP, SHAWLANDS, LINGFIELD

TQ 370 430

Shawlands was used as an emergency landing ground for aircraft during the First World War and was manned by the Pioneer Corps.

A WWII landing strip was further west on the other side of the A22.

178 PRACTICE TRENCHES AT GODSTONE

TQ 364 535

The Godstone School of Bombing constructed an elaborate series of trenches for practising trench warfare at Whitfield Plantation, Marden Park, Godstone during World War I. An interesting plan dated 1917 is extant.

179 FIRING RANGE

TQ 369 549

The scrub land below Great Church Wood, Woldingham, accommodated a firing range with retractable targets during World War I.

---

18   ICE-HOUSES

Ice-houses belong to the age before refrigerators and became in general use in Britain in the seventeenth century. Probably James I had the first British ice-house built in Greenwich Park during 1619-1620. The purpose of an ice-house was to store ice collected in the winter for use in the summer. The uses were cooling wine, making ice-cream, preserving food and for medicinal purposes. Ice-houses are generally associated with country mansions and luxury living although there were large urban ice repositories, and other massive ice stores came into being for the fishing industry.

An ice-house is an expected part of the large country estates. In winter ice was collected, usually from the nearby lake, and rammed into a solid mass in the ice-house. Insulation was effected by straw packed around the ice but mainly by the construction of the ice-house itself. It was sunk into the ground, often brick-lined and roofed over with a brick or stone dome, which was in turn covered with a thick layer of earth. Access was usually by a tunnel leading to the dome and often there was a sealable orifice in the dome. It is the hump of the dome, often with a clump of trees and situated not too far from a lake which reveals the presence of a defunct ice-house

180 ICE HOUSE AT BREWER STREET

TQ 322 515

This ice-house is at the top of a field opposite the Old Rectory. It can be identified by a group of trees. It is in a state of dereliction and has a short vaulted passage leading to a large stone-lined pit with a domed roof.

The remains of a lake which may have provided ice for the ice-house can be found lower down on the east side and adjacent to the north-south footpath.

181 ORME HOUSE SCHOOL, SOUTH GODSTONE

(FORMERLY TILBURSTOW HILL LODGE)

TQ 355 496

A damaged and decayed brick-built ice-house, can be seen built into a bank about 150 yards from the road. The interior chamber is about 3.3m in diameter and about 2.7m high.

182 ICE-HOUSE AT HOOKWOOD, LIMPSFIELD

TQ 409 534 *

The owners of the house named Hookwood discovered a buried ice-house after heavy rain had caused a crater to appear in their lawn in 1969. The chamber was of mortared sandstone and ironstone but the tunnel entrance was of good quality bricks dated to the late 17th century. There was a pond nearby.

183 ICE-HOUSE AT ICE-HOUSE WOOD ROAD, LIMPSFIELD

TQ 395 517 *

The garden at the western end, and on the north side of the road called Ice-house Wood, appears to be situated on the site of an old quarry, and the brick dome of an ice-house projects from the ground at the lowest part of the garden.

184 ICE-HOUSE AT THE MOUND, WAR COPPICE ROAD, CATERHAM

TQ 329 533

This is the site of an Iron-Age hill fort named Cardinal's Cap. It is a site of great archaeological importance which was mutilated in 1876 when a concrete house was built in oriental style. The concreting extended to the construction of an ice-house in the grounds, near the former coach house now known as Mound Cottage.

In 1993 the house is still a private residence and has claim to being the first house constructed of concrete.

---

19   BBC RECEIVING STATION, TATSFIELD

---

185 TQ 403 560 ■

This came into being in 1929 when the BBC bought land on the isolated plateau near the highest point of the North Downs from the Titsey Estate Company which handled the business of the local Leveson Gower family. The site was selected because of its freedom from electrical interference despite being relatively close to London. Thanks to the cooperation of the GPO and electricity companies it remained free of electrical interference throughout its life and there were legal agreements with neighbouring farmers restraining them from using machinery likely to cause interference. This did not prevent a dispute over an electric fence on one occasion.

Its initial purpose was to test short-wave receivers and it was first called the BBC Listening Post. Its use in general observations on short-wave broadcasting particularly from north America was soon realised and in 1933 an additional building was erected on the site for research purposes.

An activity which started at the establishment of the site and which grew in importance was that of frequency testing, especially on the short-waves. It is important that the carrier frequencies of broadcast radio (then termed wireless) transmissions are accurately maintained. In fact there were international agreements concerning broadcast transmissions accurately adhering to their allotted frequencies in order to prevent interference between stations. Tatsfield became equipped with precision measuring equipment thus allowing frequency deviations to be detected.

The Research Department started to develop new forms of frequency control equipment for the BBC in 1937. This involved transmission experiments–a curiosity in a receiving station but which apparently caused no disruption.

By 1938 Tatsfield was an established centre of great importance exciting public interest and additional land was acquired from the Leveson Gower family. The public benefited from short-wave broadcasts which were relayed from America by the following method.

As normally received on a domestic short-wave radio set the listener would encounter periodic fading of the programme he or she was listening to, accompanied by an uncomfortable increase in the volume of background noise. It was a curious fact that if two short-wave receiving sets were on at the same time normally only one faded at any given moment. Thus the fading (which was the result of the signal to the receiver from the other side of the world being affected by atmospheric conditions) could be counteracted using two or more sets. At Tatsfield two receiving sets were wired together in parallel thus overcoming the fading but the background noise was also suppressed; because the set receiving the strongest signal was made to cut out the set receiving the weaker signal and from which the background noise otherwise emanated. The improved signal reception now produced was conveyed down landlines for re-broadcasting on the BBC network.

In the interests of truth it should be said that the above was only one technique used to relay broadcasts conforming to a high quality from America. But all techniques required that the receiving set contributing the strongest signal momentarily suppressed the output of the others. Also highly directional aerials were required.

Tatsfield was used to find the best wavelengths for the British Empire Service. This involved testing propagation conditions for various wavelengths.

A most important function which started in 1938 was the monitoring of the BBC foreign language broadcasts. At one time the BBC were broadcasting in 48 different languages and it was necessary to ensure that each language was being broadcast on the correct frequency. Staff at the transmission station would not normally know which language they were broadcasting. Tatsfield employed language experts.

In the same year Tatsfield began monitoring television transmission from Alexandra Palace.

Tatsfield played a full part not only in war-time activities but also in political situations leading to WWII. For example the Italian dictator, Mussolini, would broadcast programmes from Italy purporting to be from Spain and telling lies about Spain for the purpose of inciting unrest. Tatsfield was able to pin-point the true source of the broadcast. This ability was also important during the war in locating the positions of enemy transmitters.

After the war Tatsfield acquired momentary glory in its alertness in picking up the first space-ship which was the Russian *Sputnik* launched secretly in 1957. Later when the Russian *Vostok* satellite was put into orbit Tatsfield proved that there were actually two of them by detecting messages between them.

Tatsfield started with a staff of two or three on a small site which had no water supply–rain water from the roof had to be collected. It eventually grew to a site of forty acres with full technical and recreational facilities for a staff of seventy. It was one of the first international monitoring stations in the world (Brussels, also in 1929 was the first) and its achievements are a monument to public service broadcasting. But it could not survive modern business and financial management fashions which began to come to the fore in the 1970s and (like many other industries) it closed and it's functions were transferred to BBC Caversham near Reading in Berkshire.

In 1993 only a few ruined buildings, concrete footings and anchorage points for the aerials remained. Just one small fragment remained of the wooden aerial poles. The imposing cob-web of aerials which enveloped the site including the inverted-**V** aerials which were used for the American relays were gone. At the high point south east of the station buildings a bunker still stood but it is capped with a modern aerial said to be used by a car telephone company. A small part of the site near the ruined buildings is occupied by massive pylons of a commercial broadcasting company.

20   AIR MINISTRY LIGHTHOUSE

186 TQ 405 559

The high point of the former BBC receiving station at Tatsfield is north of Clarks Lane at **46** TQ 405 559. 223 feet NNW of this was a flashing light beacon, made by Plessey and known as the lighthouse, which was employed on the alternative air route from Paris to Croydon before WWII. It was still in place (although not used) in 1941 but vanished by 1993.

Although Tandridge District remains an essentially rural area, in places like Bletchingley, South Godstone, Hurst Green and South Nutfield it is possible to find small engineering and other manufacturing firms unobtrusively at work in the background.

187 TQ 301 490   ✳

The 'acid works' as it was locally known was a relatively small business, out of place in a rural setting, and was to become more and more obtrusive to the point that it became a smelly eye sore and had to be removed.

It was established on a former brick and tile works site which had been later adapted to other industrial uses. For example during WWI, jam was sold in containers made of cardboard or 'papier mache' impregnated with wax. The tops and the bottoms of the cartons were made of tinned steel.

British wax refiners were requested to set up a reclamation plant. The company, National Reclaimers Limited, dissolved the wax from used cartons and reclaimed the wax, in the form of blocks by a distillation process. The papier mache was also recovered in a usable form.

The tin plate parts of the cartons were passed on elsewhere for recovery.

The firm of James Wilkinson and Sons Ltd. manufactured hydrofluoric acid in Sheffield but in 1925 the son (Frank Wilkinson) sold it and decided to buy the old brick and tile works site at South Nutfield to start up a new manufacturing plant as a retirement venture. The attraction was a cheap site, a railway siding, and the fact that the south east was ill-served by other manufacturers of the acid.

Hydrofluoric acid is a very dangerous substance and was manufactured, with difficulty, by the hazardous interaction of fluorspar and sulphuric acid. This process lasted until the 1950s when more critical ideas on safety at work and the presence of chemical works in growing residential areas promoted worry.

The company, Nutfield Manufacturing Company Ltd, was not entirely dependent on the manufacture of hydrofluoric acid, because it sold distilled water, battery acid (made by diluting sulphuric acid), sodium fluoride, ammonium thioglycollate for hair perms and various other (sometimes unpleasant) chemicals.

In its latter days (until 1965) the company merely diluted hydrofluoric acid provided by other companies, one of which was Imperial Smelters which was part of RTZ. A consequence was the eventual acquisition of the Nutfield Company, in 1965, by RTZ. However the site went into decline, was closed in 1984, and the plant finally demolished in 1985; the site is now a new housing estate.

The only memorials to the site are the former office buildings and neighbouring houses in Clay Lane at the entrance to the housing estate.

186: The former Air Ministry Lighthouse, Tatsfield
Photo: Roger Packham Collection

GODSTONE QUARRIES

Mushroom growing has been practised in worked-out galleries in the Godstone Mines and underground quarries.

Cultivation was started at the end of last century by (it is believed) French or Belgium growers. This ceased but a new business, Hardmass, was set up which did not survive the 1930s.

Experiments to set up a modern business principally by Col. Knowle in Arch Mine after WWII failed and Col. Knowle wrote an account of his experiences.

The quarries were chosen principally because they offered cheap available space.

The mushrooms were cultivated in long ridges of compost made from horse manure which was coated with half an inch of stone dust (casing) from the mines.

Explorers of the Godstone quarries still find traces of the industry. These includes walls which were lime-washed to sterilise the environment, water pipes and watering cans, corrugated iron sheets to protect the beds from drips and remains of the ridge beds themselves. It is also apparent that the mine itself has been modified or tidied up in places by the mushroom growers.

188 BROADHAM MUSHROOM FARM, OXTED

TQ 388 516 ■

Old mines are unsuitable places to grow mushrooms since they are difficult places to keep free of mushroom disease, and it is difficult to control essential environmental factors such as temperature and humidity or set up draught free ventilation.

Broadham mushroom farm (Blue Prince Mushrooms) which stands as a collection of sheds, had a much better chance of highly productive cultivation but could not withstand the adverse economic conditions of the 1980s and lay empty for several years.

It was reopened in 1993 by Kent Intensive Farmers with the purpose of researching and growing exotic mushrooms for the table using organic media instead of straw. The commercially sensitive nature of the work precludes details being available.

188 Broadham mushroom farm
Photo: Chris Shepheard

189 LEIGH MILL, GODSTONE

TQ 362 509 ■

This site is mentioned under water mills.

Gunpowder is a mixture of finely divided sulphur, saltpetre (potassium nitrate) and charcoal produced by grinding these ingredients together, while damp, in an incorporating mill.

Queen Elizabeth I was concerned that England depended on its gunpowder supply by importing both sulphur and saltpetre. In 1561 she therefore purchased the secret of making saltpetre from a German, Gerrard Honrick. This involved extraction from animal manure and therefore places such as stables and dovecots assumed a new importance.

Thus it was that, in 1589, George and John Evelyn and Richard Hill were licensed by the Queen to collect saltpetre throughout most of England and convert it to gunpowder. As an eventual result the Evelyns were to manufacture gunpowder at Leigh Mill up until 1636. They lost the business in that year because Samuel Cordwell and George Collins of Chilworth were appointed by Charles I as sole makers of gunpowder. Consequently the industry left Godstone.

190 BAY POND, GODSTONE
TQ 353 516   *

Leigh Mill is fed by Stratton Brook. In order to ensure their water supplies to the mill, the Evelyns dammed the little stream flowing into the Stratton Brook from the north. Thus they created a large reserve pond now known as Bay Pond or Town Pond.

24   SAWMILLS

191 QUARRY ROAD, GODSTONE
TQ 351 536   *

Timber cutting was once an important industry in Tandridge District but it has not survived. The large warehouse in Quarry Road was developed from former important sawmills which survived well into the 20th century.

192 BARN THEATRE, OXTED
TQ 393 531   *

A sawmill which once stood in Limpsfield High Street was taken down and re-erected as the Barn Theatre, Bluehouse Lane, Oxted.
See photograph inside back cover

25   ROPE MAKING

193 GODSTONE GREEN
TQ 348 515   *

Up to the 20th century there was a rope making industry on Godstone Green. Almost nothing is known about this industry but a 1905 post card shows a track running across the Green from the pond to where Ivy Mill Lane meets the A25. The card describes the track as the rope walk.

It is possible that in Felbridge rope plaiting also occurred at Rowplatt Lane.

26   IRON PEARTREE WATER

194 IRON PEARTREE HOUSE
TQ 356 488   *

Iron Peartree House, Tilburstow Hill, South Godstone acquired its name from the fact that the peartree in the garden bore iron hard fruit. In the 18th century the house became involved in a thriving trade. Water from its well was sold in London for its alleged curative properties.

27   BREWING AND OAST HOUSES

Breweries and hop gardens once thrived in areas of Tandridge such as south of Limpsfield and further west at Tilburstow Hill. No hop gardens and few breweries survive.

195 BREWHOUSE, LAGHAM MANOR, SOUTH GODSTONE
TQ 363 481   LSII ■

This is a moated manor house with 18th century brewhouse, twin oasthouse and stables. Some years ago the oasthouses were modified inside and details of the construction were covered up. **49**

195: Langham Manor brewhouse, South Godstone *Photo: Chris Shepheard*

196 OASTHOUSE, OLDHOUSE FARM, CROWHURST

TQ 402 474 ■

This red brick oasthouse with tiled cone and wooden cowl is in Caterfield Lane. The purpose of an oasthouse is to kiln dry hops.

197 OASTHOUSE, STOCKETT'S MANOR

TQ 392 504 ■

This extremely beautiful Manor House now seems to have an oasthouse incorporated into it.

198 OASTHOUSE, PIKES LANE

TQ 394 466 ■

This former oasthouse is now converted to a residence and is almost opposite the entrance to the defunct Redland Brickworks.

28   COAL TAX POSTS

After the Great Fire of London in 1666 the Corporation of London was faced with the reconstruction of the City while at the same time being in debt. Parliament helped by collecting duties on coal brought into the Port of London and certain areas around London. This was the Rebuilding Act of 1667 but there was a second Rebuilding Act of 1670 which imposed higher duties. The money raised was largely intended for the reconstruction of St. Paul's and 51 other churches.

A financial crisis of 1672 caused, among other disasters, the loss of trust funds held by the Corporation of London on behalf of the orphans of City Freemen. Parliament then passed an Act for the Relief of the Orphans and other Creditors of the City of London in 1694. This extended the duties on coal but also authorised a duty on wines brought into the Port of London.

From 1767 the duties were used to finance a variety of building projects in London and by 1862 most of the duties were transferred to the Metropolitan Board of Works who were undertaking large schemes such as London's new sewage system.

The Coal Duties Act of 1845 defined the boundaries for the coal duties, as the circumference of a circle with radius of 20 miles and its centre at the General Post Office in London.

A further Act of 1851, the Coal Duties Act, made many changes and authorised the Corporation to

set up boundary marks where any road, public highway, railway and canal crossed the limit.
In 1861 the London Coal and Wine Duties Continuance Act (24 & 25 Vict. Cap. 42) altered the area to which the duties applied, to coincide with the Metropolitan Police District. The squarish hollow cast-iron posts bearing the City of London's Arms, found at road and track sides in Tandridge District should all bear the inscription 24 & 25 Vict. Cap. 42 and date to 1861. The fact that few do, is the result of a manufacturing error which were corrected with bolted-on plates but they have mostly fallen off.
The duties continued to raise money to finance civil engineering projects in London until 5 July 1890. Its discontinuance was the result of the London Coal Duties Abolition Act of 9 July 1889.

199–205 COAL TAX POSTS, WARLINGHAM LSII

(**Site 199**, TQ 371 591 ✳) On south west side of Harrow Road at junction with Chelsham Road. It is a rusty post but the inscription is intact. On parish boundary.

(**Site 200**, TQ 365 597 ✳) Just beyond the Harrow Inn where Old Farleigh Road begins.

(**Site 201**, TQ 368 596 ✳) At north east end of Daniels Lane in the undergrowth where the lane degenerates into footpaths and a bridleway. It is a rusty dilapidated post with a damaged inscription. On the parish boundary.

(**Site 202**, TQ 365 582 ✳) On west side of Chelsham Road at junction with Limpsfield Road. Adjacent to site of the former bus station and due to be re-sited in 1994. The post is near but not on parish boundary and is rusty and the inscription is spoiled.

(**Site 203**, TQ 366 584 ✳) On north east side of Sunny Banks at road junction with Chelsham Road. It is a rusty post, on the parish boundary, with a damaged inscription. The inscription on the base (normally earthed over) reads: **REGENTS CANAL IRON WORKS, HENRY CRISSELL, 1861, LONDON**. The post was slightly repositioned when work on the road junction occurred.

(**Site 204**, TQ 354 570 ✳) On north east side of Stuart Road at junction with Woldingham Road. Opposite Viaduct Lodge. It is rusty post with its erroneous inscription intact but it is half buried.

(**Site 205**, TQ 358 577 ✳) Outside house 'Waterendlath' on Bug Hill. Very prominent and the correcting plate is intact.

206–209 COAL TAX POSTS, WHYTELEAFE LSII

(**Site 206**, TQ 344 577 ✳) In Well Farm Road at bottom of bank on north side just below viaduct. Almost completely buried.

(**Site 207**, TQ 337 584 ✳) In Whyteleafe Hill a few metres north east of junction with Hornchurch Hill. It is a rusty post with an intact inscription and not too far from the former Greater London Boundary.

(**Site 208**, TQ 341 579 ✳) This post is outside 376 Godstone Road and part of the inscription (the 2(?) of the 24) has rusted right through.

(**Site 209**, TQ 340 581 ✳) The 1851 Act authorised boundary posts to be erected on railway lines. These were 4.3m (14ft) high and the Whyteleafe one which is south of Whyteleafe Station is made of stone.

203: Coal tax post   *Photo: Chris Shepheard*

210 Rev JOHN FLAMSTEED 1646-1719
TQ 312 412 ✱

In 1685 John Flamsteed became Rector of Burstow and is buried in the chancel of Burstow church.

Previous to being presented to the living at Burstow he had made himself an expert on astronomy and applied himself to the problem of determining longitude. The absence of such knowledge imperilled ships out of sight of land. Convincing King Charles II that the first step was to compile an accurate star catalogue and tables of the moon's motions he was made the first Astronomer Royal and Greenwich Observatory was built for him in 1676.

Struggling against underfunding, lack of basic facilities, lack of instrumentation and ill health Flamsteed devoted the rest of his life to his observations and his work was published six years after his death as, *Historia Coelestis Britannica*.

Flamsteed provided ground work for Isaac Newton and deserves to be recognised as one of the founding fathers of modern astronomy.

211 Sir JOSEPH WILSON SWAN
1826-1914
TQ 353 590 ✱

Joseph Swan is buried in the graveyard of All Saints Warlingham. He invented the incandescent electric bulb in 1860 — 20 years before Edison. He also invented the dry plate and bromide paper photographic process and was the first to produce a usable form of artificial silk.

FURTHER READING

Cleere, H and Crossley, D — *The Iron Industry of the Weald.* Leicester University Press, 1985

Farries, K G and Mason, M T — *The windmills of Surrey and Inner London.* Charles Skilton Ltd. London, 1966

Flint, Peter — *RAF Kenley.* Terence Dalton Limited, 1985 .

Kidner, R W — *The Oxted Line.* The Oakwood Press, 1972 revised 1981

Kidner, R W — *The Reading to Tonbridge Line.* The Oakwood Press, 1974

Lambert, Uvedale — *Godstone. A Short History.* 1982

Maggs, Ken and De'Athe, Paul — *The Roman Roads of East Surrey and the Kent Border.* North Downs Press, 1987

Robert H S Robinson. — *Fuller's earth: A history of calcium montmorillonite.* Volturna Press, Hythe, Kent, 1986

Skuse, Peter R — *A History of Whyteleafe.* The Bourne Society, 1987

Stidder, D — *The Water Mills of Surrey.* Barracuda Books, 1990

Tait, Geoffry — *Redhill at War. The lighter side.* G Tait and Associates Ltd. Warlingham.

The Bourne Society's *Local History Records*.

ABOUT THE AUTHOR

Malcolm Tadd was born in Brighton and spent his working life in industrial chemistry and information science. He is chiefly noted for being president of the Wealden Cave and Mine Society and secretary of Subterranea Britannica which exists to promote the study of man-made and man-used underground structures as an important branch of archaeology.

Industrial archaeology is a parallel passion.

Malcolm is normally to be found walking the countryside, entering or emerging from holes in the ground, or exploring the back streets of towns and cities with Barbara Tadd.